# Living with a
# Chihuahua

### Edited by Margaret Greening

**BARRON'S**

**THE QUESTION OF GENDER**
*The "he" pronoun is used throughout this book in favor of the rather impersonal "it," but no gender bias is intended at all.*

## ACKNOWLEDGMENTS
The publisher would like to thank the following for help with photography: Margaret Greening (Hamaja), Pat Cullen (Culcia), Brenda Hayes (Ardenvale), Diana Grant (Elmington), Shirley Orme (Ormeslet), Sylvia Fresson (Teocali), and Carol Davies (Dachida's).

First edition for the United States and Canada published in 2003 by Barron's Educational Series, Inc.

First published in 2003 by Interpet Publishing
*Living with a Chihuahua*
Copyright © 2003 Ringpress Books

All rights reserved.
No part of this book may be reproduced in any form, by photostat, microfilm, xerography, or any other means, or incorporated into any information retrieval system, electronic or mechanical, without the written permission of the copyright owner.

*All inquiries should be addressed to:*
Barron's Educational Series, Inc.
250 Wireless Boulevard
Hauppauge, New York 11788
**http://www.barronseduc.com**

*Library of Congress Catalog Card No. 2002112505*

International Standard Book No. 0-7641-5636-5

Printed and bound in Singapore
9 8 7 6 5 4 3 2

# CONTENTS

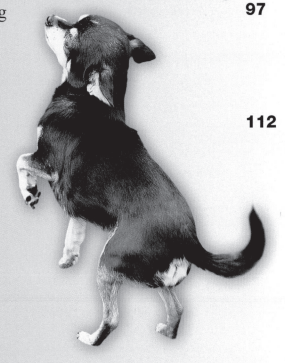

# CHAPTER ONE

# INTRODUCING THE CHIHUAHUA

**B**right, alert, inquisitive, loyal, and affectionate, the tiny Chihuahua – the smallest of all dogs – has it all. This is a breed that is big on personality, and despite being no more than a few inches tall, the Chihuahua is ready to take on the world.

Like all the Toy breeds, the Chihuahua is first and foremost a companion dog, and comes under the umbrella title of being a "lapdog." He fits this description in the sense that he loves people, and is only too happy to be cuddled on a lap. However, it would be a mistake to think that this is all a Chihuahua does.

This is a highly intelligent little dog who thrives on having things to do. He is interested in everything that is going on, and is always eager to get involved. The Chihuahua can be trained to a high level, and representatives of the breed have made their mark in a number of different disciplines, including Competitive Obedience, Flyball, and Agility. The loving Chihuahua is the perfect therapy dog, bringing comfort to both children and adults in need, and, as an added bonus, he takes the show ring by storm. This is a breed that is full of surprises, and once you have owned a Chihuahua, no other breed will do.

## SECRET HISTORY

One of the most fascinating aspects of the dog world is discovering the origins of the hundreds of different breeds. The Chihuahua must win the prize for having the most mysterious history, which is a mixture of legend, folklore, and documentary evidence. We cannot even be certain which country the breed came from, as there are two schools of thought, each with its own band of supporters.

## THE MEXICAN CHIHUAHUA

The Chihuahua could be one of a handful of native American breeds, with roots in the early civilizations of Central America and Mexico.

*The Techichi dog, a possible ancestor of the Chihuahua, was thought to have special, mystical powers.*

This theory is supported by the evidence of Toltec carvings, which date back to the ninth century A.D. These show a small dog, with a round head and large, erect ears, called the Techichi, who strongly resembles the modern Chihuahua.

The Toltecs were conquered by the Aztecs, who developed one of the most sophisticated civilizations in the world. It was famous for art, culture, learning, and architecture. But the lives of the Aztecs were dominated by religion. Their chief aim was to appease the gods with ceremonial sacrifices – and these included humans as well as animals. The human "victims" lived a life of luxury until the fateful day, and it is thought that the animals were treated in a similar way.

The Techichi dogs lived in temples and were cared for by the priests. They were prized for their special mystical powers and were thought to have the ability to see into the future. They were also famed for their healing power, with the belief that they cured disease by absorbing it into themselves, or by passing it to someone else. When the time came for a blood offering, these dogs were sacrificed in large numbers.

The red Techichi had a very special role in the Aztecs' view of the afterlife. They believed he could guide the souls of the dead to the underworld, making the journey across the river that separated the living world from the world of the dead. Because of these special powers, it became the custom to kill a Techichi when someone died, and to bury him with the human

remains. This legend is borne out by fact –
many graves that have been excavated in Mexico
have contained the skeletons of small dogs.

The Aztecs were conquered by the Spanish in
the sixteenth century, and little more was heard
of the Techichi. It could be that the dogs went
feral, living off small rodents, but this is only
speculation. There is an interval of more than
300 years before documented evidence comes
to light.

## THE MEDITERRANEAN CHIHUAHUA

The other theory concerning the origins of the
Chihuahua puts the breed in another part of the
world.

Small lapdogs have lived in Europe for many,
many centuries, and it is thought that ancestors
of the Chihuahua may have become established
on the island of Malta. It is known that dogs
with the molera trait (an open fontanel – see
page 18), which is unique to Chihuahuas, lived
on the island.

Trading ships visited Malta, and some of the
island dogs were taken to other parts of Europe.
We can see evidence of this in many of the
European paintings of the period, particularly in
a fresco by Sandro Botticelli, which was created
around 1482. The theme of the fresco is the life
of Moses, but it clearly shows a small dog of
Chihuahua type, with a round head, big eyes,
and large, erect ears.

This is the strongest evidence of the
Mediterranean Chihuahua, for the fresco is
dated before Christopher Columbus sailed to
the New World.

## DISCOVERING THE CHIHUAHUA

We now leap forward to the 1850s, abandoning
myth and legend, to the time when small dogs
were discovered in Mexico. They came in a
variety of coat types – long, short, and even
hairless, which eventually became known as the
Mexican Hairless.

The small dogs were taken to the United
States, where, initially, they were known as
Arizona Dogs or Texas Dogs. Later, the

*The longhaired variety has an enthusiastic
following.*

longhaired and shorthaired varieties were rechristened Mexican Chihuahuas, after the Mexican state where they were discovered.

In 1884, the breed made its show ring debut when it was exhibited in the Miscellaneous Class as a Chihuahua Terrier. The first Chihuahua to be registered by the American Kennel Club was Midget, born in 1903 and owned by H. Raynor of El Paso, Texas. Numbers crept up gradually, with 50 Chihuahuas shown at AKC events in 1916. But then the breed took off in dramatic fashion, reaching 37,000 registrations in 1967. Since then, the breed has remained among the top 20 ratings, and in 2001 it came in as the ninth most popular breed in the United States, with a total of 38,926 registrations.

British dog fanciers were fascinated by the tiny Toy breed that was all the rage in America, and the breed was quickly adopted in the UK and throughout the rest of the world. In 2002, English Kennel Club registrations were 1,279.

## TWO VARIETIES

The modern Chihuahua comes in two varieties: long coat and smooth coat. Most breed enthusiasts see the smooth coat as the original Chihuahua, and it has always been the most popular of the two varieties in the United States. The long-coated type has been interbred with other Toy dogs, such as the Papillon, but now this variety is strongly established as a separate entity. Today, the long coat and the smooth coat are shown in separate classes, but apart from length of coat, the varieties are identical in both character and conformation.

## COMPANION PAR EXCELLENCE

The Chihuahua is now on a firm footing on both sides of the Atlantic, and, perhaps most important, the breed is valued for the right reasons. There is a novelty in owning the world's smallest dog, but there are far more important considerations. Today, the Chihuahua is a slightly bigger, heavier dog than it once was,

*Fun-loving, intelligent, and affectionate – the Chihuahua is the breed that has it all…*

but this has resulted in a major improvement in its overall health. This can only be good news for the breed.

Now we have a Toy dog that is a wonderful companion, and is small enough to go everywhere. He is exceptionally loyal to his owners, and, despite his size, he is a mini guard dog, as he will be quick to bark if strangers approach. He is often described as having terrierlike qualities, and this can be seen in his fearless, outgoing nature. For a Chihuahua, life is a source of endless fascination: he wants to know about everything that is going on, and, if possible, he wants to be in the thick of the action. After a hectic period of activity, the Chihuahua is ready to rest, and he likes nothing better than to curl up in a lap, on a soft cushion, or alongside a fellow companion.

If you decide that the Chihuahua is the breed for you, remember that you must cater to all his needs, both mental and physical. A small dog should not be pampered and overindulged; he should be taken seriously as a dog who enjoys the full range of canine activities. If you treat him as such, you will be rewarded with a happy, loyal dog that will provide you with years of loving companionship – and endless entertainment!

*The Chihuahua may be the world's smallest dog, but he has a powerful brain, which he likes to use.*

# CHAPTER TWO

# PUPPY POWER

Chihuahuas are among the most appealing of all dog breeds, and Chihuahua puppies are irresistible. However, it is important that you not succumb to temptation and rush into Chihuahua ownership before giving it serious consideration. You may think that a small dog is easy to care for, but, in fact, the responsibility and commitment is exactly the same as if you were taking on an Irish Wolfhound!

Ask yourself the following questions:

**Am I prepared to care for a dog from the moment he arrives in my home until the end of his life?** Remember, the Chihuahua is a long-lived breed, and most will live into their teens.

**Can I afford to keep a Chihuahua?** A small dog is not going to cost a lot to feed, but there may be times when you want to go away and will have to pay for boarding kennels. Veterinary fees are also a consideration.

**Am I prepared to find the time to train and socialize my Chihuahua?** A dog will become a good companion only if he is taught how to behave in all situations.

**Will I be a suitable companion for my Chihuahua?** This is a breed that thrives on human companionship, and a dog will pine if he is left alone for long periods. The maximum period a dog should be left alone is four hours – regardless of the breed.

**Is my family setup right for a Chihuahua?** If you have very small children, a Chihuahua is not a good choice. A tiny dog could easily get injured in the rough and tumble of family life. Most breeders will not sell a puppy to a family that has children under eight years of age – and some breeders may be even more prohibitive.

*The Chihuahua is an excellent family dog, as long as children are of a suitable age.*

**If I already have a dog, is he likely to get along with a Chihuahua?** If you already own a Chihuahua, there is no problem, as Chihuahuas seem to relate well to others of their kind. If you have a bigger breed, you must be confident that your dog is well trained and will not take advantage of a small dog (see The Resident Dog, page 30).

If you have considered the above points, and feel confident that you can provide a suitable home for a Chihuahua, the next task is to track down a puppy.

### FINDING A BREEDER
The best plan is to contact the AKC for a list of breed clubs. The breed club secretary will have a list of breeders, and they may even know who has puppies available.

You may also find it helpful to visit a dog show so that you can see lots of different representatives of the breed. After showing is over, most exhibitors will be happy to talk about their dogs and to answer any questions.

When you have found a breeder who has a litter of puppies, you will need to make some decisions about the type of dog you want.

### MALE OR FEMALE?
Pet owners often prefer a female puppy, believing she will be less trouble than her male counterpart, and will also be more affectionate. In fact, the Chihuahua male often relates better to people, particularly to women. A male Chihuahua enjoys attention, but he is also confident and self-contained.

*The Chihuahua expresses his character in many different ways.*

The rule of thumb with female Chihuahuas is that they are all different! They share the typical Chihuahua characteristics of being lively, loving, and inquisitive, but these may be expressed in different ways. Some are friends with everyone, some gravitate toward one person, others prefer men. Generally, females tend to be a little more independent in their outlook than males.

However, regardless of gender, a Chihuahua from sound breeding will be a loyal and affectionate companion.

If you choose a female, you will need to cope with her seasonal cycle. A mature Chihuahua will come into season every eight to nine months, and during this time she must be kept away from male dogs or you will risk an accidental mating. Many people spay their female pets.

## MORE THAN ONE?

You may be tempted to buy a couple of Chihuahuas so that they will be company for each other.

With bigger breeds, it is not a good idea to buy two pups from the same litter, as it is difficult to give either dog enough attention. However, Chihuahuas are independent little dogs, and will generally get as much attention as they ask for. They will enjoy the canine company, but will still be focused on their human family.

Two males will usually get along best together, but Chihuahuas seem to like living as a little tribe, and arguments between dogs of any sex are usually few and far between.

## COAT TYPE

The Chihuahua has two coat types: long and smooth. The long-coated Chihuahua is often more popular with pet owners, but it should be remembered that this coat is more labor-intensive. The feathering around the ears and the tail will mat and tangle unless it is groomed on a daily basis. The smooth-coated Chihuahua is obviously easier to care for, and will look smart with routine grooming (see page 71).

Breeders often specialize in either long-coated or smooth-coated Chihuahuas, so you will need to make up your mind about coat type before tracking down a litter.

There has been no interbreeding between purebred long-coated and smooth-coated Chihuahuas for many years, but occasionally a long-coated pup will appear in a "smooth-coated" litter (caused by a recessive gene). By the age of five weeks, the coat type will have become obvious.

*Coat type will be obvious by the time the puppies are five weeks old.*

*A blue Chihuahua may be harder to find.*

## COLOR

One of the delights of the breed is that the Chihuahua can be any color. For the pet owner, this is purely a matter of personal preference, although some colors, such as blue, may be harder to find than others. In the show ring, cream, fawn, and white are the most popular colors, although a black and tan Chihuahua can look very smart. A parti-colored dog, which has broken patches of color, is more likely to succeed in the American show ring than in the UK.

## SHOW POTENTIAL

Are you planning to exhibit your Chihuahua in the show ring? If you are interested in becoming involved with this aspect of dog ownership, you need to find a puppy with show potential. The breeder will give you guidance, or you can ask an experienced Chihuahua breeder to view the litter and give an objective opinion (see Puppy to Champion, page 107).

## SIZE MATTERS

The Breed Standard, the written blueprint for the breed, states that the Chihuahua should not exceed 6 lb (2.7 kg). The English Standard states a preference for dogs that weigh 2–4 lb (1–1.8 kg).

In reality, most dogs in the ring are 4 lb or more, and a really "tiny" Chihuahua is becoming increasingly rare. This is for the good of the breed, as very small Chihuahuas have shown a tendency to increased health problems – they are more frail, tend to have shorter life expectancies, and can have heart conditions. If a breeder has a particularly small puppy, it should go to an experienced Chihuahua owner, because it will need special care.

If you choose a female Chihuahua and plan to breed from her, you must make sure that she is of a reasonable size so that she will be able to carry a litter of puppies. (See Chapter Seven: Seeking Perfection.)

## AN OLDER DOG

You may be in a situation where it would be difficult to care for a puppy but you are able to cope with an older dog. Sometimes, a breeder will "run on" a couple of puppies to see how they develop. If a dog proves to be unsuitable for showing, the breeder will look for a suitable pet home. A dog that has been retired from showing, or from breeding, may also be available to a pet home.

If you take on an older dog, you will need to be especially patient and considerate to begin with. An adult will be used to his old home, and will take a little time to settle in.

For information on rescued dogs, see Chapter Five.

## ASSESSING THE LITTER

The breeder will usually invite potential buyers to view a litter when the puppies are around five weeks of age. At this stage the pups will be up on their feet, so you will see how they move, and how they interact with each other.

Because of their size, Chihuahuas do not have big litters, and the average size is two to three puppies. However, there are always exceptions, such as the Chihuahua who successfully produced two litters, each containing six puppies.

When you go to see the breeder, look for the following signs:

- The puppies should be in a clean, fresh-smelling environment. Droppings should be cleaned up, and there should be no evidence of leftover food.
- The puppies should be well covered, but certainly not fat.

- The coat should be clean, with no sign of dandruff.
- The eyes should be bright, with no evidence of discharge.
- The ears should be clean, and free from bad odor. The Chihuahua carries his ears in an erect position, and if a pup is to have the correct ear carriage, this should be apparent at around eight weeks of age. (See Teething, page 38.)
- The rear of the pup should be clean. Any sign of fecal matter may indicate diarrhea.

It is important to see the mother with her puppies, as this will give you an idea of temperament. The mother may not be looking her best, as she has been nursing a litter of puppies. The long-coated Chihuahua will "drop" her coat after having a litter, so do not be surprised if she is looking a bit sparse. The smooth-coated Chihuahua will also drop her coat, but the effect is less dramatic. Regardless

*The mother should be happy to show off her babies.*

*The puppies should appear to be lively and inquisitive.*

## THE MOLERA

The molera, or open fontanel, is a trait peculiar to Chihuahuas. It can be felt as a soft spot on the top of the dog's head. In other breeds (and in human babies), the frontal and parietal bones of the cranium fuse soon after birth. In some Chihuahuas, this process may take a lot longer, or the bones may never fuse completely. It is reckoned that the bones will fuse in 50 percent of Chihuahuas born with this condition, by the age of three.

Research has shown that a Chihuahua with a molera is perfectly healthy, although the dog should be treated with a little more care, as the head is more vulnerable.

of this, the mother should look fit and healthy, and she should be happy to show off her puppies.

You will probably not be able to see the puppies' father. In most cases, the stud dog will belong to another breeder. However, you may be able to see a photo of him. Ideally, you will be able to view some adults that are related to the puppies. This will give you some clue as to how the pups will turn out in terms of both appearance and temperament.

Generally, the adults and the puppies should show the alert, inquisitive nature that is so typical of the Chihuahua. Some dogs will rush up to greet you, whereas others may be slightly more wary in their approach.

However, once introductions have been made, a Chihuahua of sound temperament should be quite happy to make your acquaintance.

## THE BIG DECISION

All puppies look irresistible, and you may well

*The breeder will help you to pick a puppy that is most likely to suit your lifestyle.*

*The Chihuahua loves his creature comforts, so buying a cozy bed should be a top priority.*

find that it is hard to make a choice. The breeder will have watched the pups closely since they were born, and will be able to help you find the pup that is most likely to fit in with your lifestyle. Some puppies are bolder than others, and this is the type that would thrive in a family. A shy puppy, that needs bringing out, should go to a quieter home, ideally with an experienced owner who can give the pup special attention.

When you have made your decision, you will generally be asked to pay a deposit, and the pup will be ready to collect when he is around ten weeks old.

## GETTING READY
It may seem like a long wait before your puppy is ready to come home, but you can use the time getting ready for the new arrival.

### Buying Equipment
Dogs do not need lots of expensive equipment, but there are a few essential purchases.

### Bed and Bedding
The Chihuahua loves his creature comforts, so a cozy bed should be considered a necessity. There are lots of different dog beds to choose from, and it is largely a matter of personal choice. The most practical option is a hard plastic bed. This is easy to clean, and it can withstand chewing. If it is lined with fleece bedding, it makes a perfect doggy home.

If you decide to go for a bed made out of fabric, make sure it can be washed without too much trouble.

### Crate/Carrier
A crate, or carrier, is a multipurpose piece of equipment that is well worth the investment.

If a Chihuahua is trained to go into his crate or travel carrier (see page 34), he will learn to see it as his own special den where he can feel safe and secure. The crate can be used in the car, and it can be used as a portable home when you are going away.

Make sure that the crate you buy is big

enough for an adult Chihuahua to be comfortable. As a rough guide, it should be 12 inches wide, 18–24 inches long, and 12–14 inches high (30 x 45–60 x 30–35 cm). If you opt for a travel carrier, avoid those that open from the top. The Chihuahua seems to dislike the lid effect, and has a tendency to jump out as soon as the door is opened.

You will also need to buy some bedding so you can make the crate as cozy as possible.

### Bowls

You will need two bowls: one for food and one for drinking water. There are plenty to choose from. Do not buy anything that is too big, and beware of lightweight plastic bowls that can be easily chewed.

### Collar and Lead

A Chihuahua puppy will not be happy if you try to fit him with a bulky collar and a heavyweight lead. Choose a lightweight, adjustable, nylon collar, and a thin lead that has a secure trigger fastening. The other option is to buy a show lead, which is both a collar and a lead. This is easy to slip on, and is very lightweight. It is probably best to use this for training sessions at home, rather than using it when you go out.

### ID

When your puppy is ready to go out in public, he will need to have some form of identification. This can take the form of a license tag, engraved with your contact details. Or you may prefer to go for a permanent form of ID, such as a

*All dogs should have some form of ID.*

microchip implant. This is a straightforward procedure and can be carried out by a veterinarian during a routine visit.

### Grooming Gear

To begin with, all you need is a soft baby brush so that you can get your puppy accustomed to being groomed. If you are getting a long-coated puppy, you will also need to get a comb. For information on handling and grooming a puppy, see pages 40–42. For information on grooming the adult Chihuahua, see pages 71–78.

### Toys

Toys are fun to buy, and, if your puppy has his own things to play with, he will not be so destructive in the home. Make sure the toys you buy are 100 percent safe. A dog can be seriously harmed if he chews up a toy and swallows the bits.

## IN THE HOME

The first job is to decide where your puppy is going to sleep. Most people choose the kitchen or a utility room, but it is a matter of personal choice. The only proviso is that the bed should be located somewhere that is warm and free from drafts.

When you have sorted out the sleeping arrangements, you can check the rest of the house to ensure that it is as puppy-proofed as possible. Your pup will make a beeline for trailing curtains and tablecloths, and he will be quick to investigate the fringes on carpets and furniture. Houseplants are a great source of temptation, and trailing electric wires are a very real hazard.

The best plan is to try to see your home from a puppy's viewpoint – and then put away anything that is valuable or potentially dangerous.

## IN THE YARD

Do not make the mistake of thinking that a tiny Chihuahua will be safe in your yard. This is a breed that has endless curiosity and will be all too ready to disappear through a gap in the fence. It is essential to make sure that your yard is securely fenced, right down to the ground, and check that the gate shuts securely. Generally, a fence of 2 feet, 6 inches (76 cm) should be sufficient for all but the most determined escapologist.

Some Chihuahuas have a gift for climbing, and they really can pose a problem for their owners. If you have a "climber," you will

*A Chihuahua puppy will investigate everything – so make sure your yard is safe...*

have to increase the height of your fencing and make sure your Chihuahua is not left unsupervised in the yard.

If your neighbors keep a dog, it is important to have solid fencing; otherwise the dogs may be tempted to "run the fence" barking at each other.

Some plants are poisonous to dogs, and you would be advised to ask an expert to check your yard. A number of insecticides are also toxic, so you will need to take extra care once your puppy arrives home.

## FINDING A VETERINARIAN

The veterinarian will be a very important person in your Chihuahua's life, so it is important to find a practice that you are happy with. Before you get your puppy, check out the veterinary practices in the area and find out which is the most suitable. Ideally, you want a veterinarian who has particular experience with Chihuahuas.

Fortunately, the Chihuahua is generally healthy and long-lived, but there are some health issues associated with the breed, which your vet should be aware of. (See Chapter Eight: Health Care.)

### Choosing a Name

While you are waiting for your puppy, you can choose a name for him. Doubtless, this will be a source of great debate among family and friends – but make up your mind before the puppy arrives home. More than one dog has gone through life being called Puppy because of the owner's indecision!

*Choose your puppy's name before he arrives home.*

Here are some points to bear in mind when choosing a name:

- It should be short (no more than a couple of syllables).
- It should be easy to say.
- It should be instantly recognizable.
- It should not be a joke name – the joke will wear very thin over the next decade or so.

If your puppy is registered with the AKC or another national kennel club, the breeder may have allocated a show name, but you will still be able to choose a call name.

### COLLECTING YOUR PUPPY

At last the waiting is over, and it is time to pick up your puppy. If you are traveling by car, it is best to go with a friend or a member of the family so that one person can drive while the other concentrates on the puppy. Otherwise, be sure to take a carrier.

Bring some towels for the puppy to cuddle up in, and take some paper towels in case of accidents. If you have a long journey, or if it is a hot day, you should take some drinking water and a bowl. If possible, arrange to pick up your puppy early in the day, so that you have plenty of time to settle him into his new home.

The breeder will probably have a "puppy pack" ready for you. This should include the following:

*At last, the time has come for you to collect your puppy.*

- a copy of the puppy's pedigree
- paperwork from the AKC or another national kennel club for transfer of ownership
- details of when the pup has been wormed, and when the next treatment is due
- details of inoculations (the timing of which will depend on what country you live in, your veterinarian's policy, and what age you take the puppy)
- a diet sheet, giving information on type of food, quantity, and number of meals a day
- a sample of food. Most breeders will supply enough food to last a couple of days (see pages 24 and 37)
- contact details so that you can seek advice if necessary.

## THE JOURNEY HOME

In most cases, your puppy will make a few token protests, and will then settle down to sleep for the journey home. Remember, if you have to stop, your puppy should not be allowed on the ground (in case he picks up a disease).

## SETTLING IN

Try to imagine what it is like for a puppy to arrive in a new home. He has left familiar surroundings, and he has been parted from his brothers and sisters. For the first time, he is facing life on his own – and it is all completely different from what he has been used to.

*Start by giving the pup a chance to explore his new surroundings.*

*Give lots of reassurance to help boost your puppy's confidence.*

## FEEDING

You can offer your puppy a meal, using the food sample that has been provided by the puppy's breeder. At first, you may find that your pup is reluctant to eat. There is so much going on that it is hard to concentrate on one thing, and your puppy may also miss the rivalry of feeding with his littermates.

If you have a reluctant feeder, give your pup five minutes to eat what he wants, and then remove the bowl. Make sure fresh drinking water is available, and try not to worry too much if the pup has only picked at his food. He will probably eat more at his next meal, and will gradually return to eating his full rations. Always provide fresh food at each meal, so it is as appetizing as possible.

If you are concerned about your puppy's appetite, or if he has a stomach upset that does not clear up within 24 hours, consult your vet.

## THE FIRST NIGHT

This is the moment you have been dreading – settling the puppy for the night, and then listening to his howls of protest!

First of all, you must make a firm decision as to where your Chihuahua is going to sleep. If you are happy to allow your dog to sleep on your bed, or in your bedroom, that is fine. But if you would prefer to have a dog that sleeps in his own bed, in his own sleeping quarters, you must be firm.

If you are using a crate, your task will be easier, as you know your puppy is safely confined, and cannot get into mischief (see

Start by taking your puppy out to the yard. This will give him the opportunity to stretch his legs after the journey, and to relieve himself. When your pup "performs," give him lots of praise. Start as you mean to go on!

Next, take your puppy into the house and show him where his bed is. Give the pup a chance to sniff around and explore while you give gentle praise and encouragement.

It is very tempting to invite your friends and neighbors to see the new arrival, but this should be resisted. Give your puppy a chance to first meet the members of his new family so that he can figure out who he belongs to.

*Try to resist your puppy's cries on the first night. If he is left, he will soon learn to settle.*

Crate Training, page 34). If your pup is to be left in the kitchen or utility room, and is not in a crate, make a thorough check to ensure that the room is puppy-proofed.

At bedtime, take your puppy out to relieve himself, settle him down in his bed with a couple of treats, and then close the door on him. You can try leaving a radio playing with the volume turned low, as some puppies seem to be reassured by the sound.

Try to resist the temptation of going to comfort your Chihuahua when he cries. All he will learn is that crying brings results – and the more he cries, the better the chance of being "rescued."

In most cases, exhaustion will take over, and a puppy who has spent the day exploring his home will need a good sleep.

If you stick to this routine for a couple of nights, your Chihuahua will accept that he is left on his own at nighttime, and will understand that he must settle until morning.

# CHAPTER THREE

# THE RIGHT START

O nce your puppy has got over the trauma of moving home, you will need to establish a routine to suit a growing Chihuahua. You will need to sort out diet, exercise, and grooming requirements, as well as make a start on your puppy's education and socialization. It is easy to think that a tiny Chihuahua puppy cannot cope with "lessons," but this is far from being the case. A young puppy is tremendously receptive; he soaks up new experiences like a sponge, so there is no sense in delaying his training.

## GETTING ALONG WITH CHILDREN

Toy breeds are not the best choice if you have small children, and it would be a mistake to take on a Chihuahua if you have children below the age of eight.

However, if you have older children, a Chihuahua can fit in very well with family life, providing introductions are closely supervised, and the children are taught a sense of responsibility.

- Ask the children to sit on the floor, and let them have a turn at holding the puppy. It is best if all interactions between the puppy and the children take place at ground level, because then there is no danger of the pup being dropped.
- Provide each child with a small treat to give to the pup, and make sure the puppy takes it gently.
- Over the next few days, you can supervise some play sessions, using one of your puppy's new toys. Make sure that the games are not too rough, and that the puppy gives up his toy willingly at the end of a game.

The children must learn to respect the puppy as a living being. The pup should be allowed to rest when he is tired, and he should never be teased. The puppy, in turn, must learn that the

*Supervise all interactions with children to begin with.*

smaller members of his family must be obeyed.

When your puppy has settled, you can encourage the children to help with his daily care. Under supervision, a child can prepare meals, groom the pup, and work at simple training exercises (see Chapter Four: Training Targets). This encourages the child to be responsible, and it will also help to build a rewarding relationship between child and dog.

Even if you do not have children, it is important to work at this aspect of your Chihuahua's training. Beg, borrow, or steal some children who are used to dogs, and supervise a couple of play sessions. Your Chihuahua needs to become accustomed to children, so that he is not worried or frightened by them when he meets them in a public place.

## MUMMY MUNECA

Danna Ceja, from California, has owned Chihuahuas since she was a 12-year-old child, and firmly believes that, with careful supervision and training, there is no reason why Chihuahuas and children cannot become the best of friends.

"My two sons, Erick and Rafael (Ralphie), were 14 and 11 respectively when Muneca joined our household. The boys accepted her straightaway, and she them, although she very quickly assumed the role of 'tattletale,' running downstairs to attract my attention if she thought the boys were doing something they shouldn't, which was most of the time! When I told them off, she would stand there, wagging her tail.

"Later, we acquired Diamond, a male Chihuahua, and my two boys were very excited about his arrival. This was partly because Diamond was to be a show dog, unlike Muneca, and also because he was a boy – I think it's some kind of macho, male-bonding thing. Diamond bonded immediately with Erick and Ralphie, and they would play for hours together.

"The boys have always loved the dogs, and been active in caring for them. When my youngest son was 18, I had a bitch called Salsa who was expecting a litter. During the night, she went into labor. For some reason, she would not nibble off the umbilical cords of her puppies and I had to cut them. I needed help for this, so I woke up my son and got him to help. I asked him to hold the puppies while I tied and cut the umbilical cords. Erick had to go to the bathroom three times, he was so revolted by the experience. His comment was, 'Mom, this is so gross!' Despite this, however, he stayed to help with all the other puppies. I was very proud of him.

"My sons are grown up now, and I have a wonderful grandson. His name is also Rafael, but we always call him Moe, after one of the Three Stooges. Moe has been adopted by my

*The playful Chihuahua delights in a child's company, as long as both learn a sense of mutual respect.*

Chis. When Moe came home from the hospital, Ralphie and his wife brought Moe to meet me. Moe was put on the sofa, still in his baby seat, and straightaway, Muneca came to investigate the new arrival. She jumped into the baby seat with him and snuggled down by his side. Moe was born prematurely, and weighed only five pounds, and Muneca was a tiny four pounds, so there was ample room for both of them in the baby seat. Muneca was instantly very protective of this new little human, and wouldn't let my son or his wife near the baby. At the time, I was in another room, and I only saw what had happened when I heard a cry of, 'Moaaaaam! Muneca won't let us get our baby!' Once I had retrieved Moe, and let Muneca have a good sniff of him, there were no more problems, but Muneca still protects Moe, who I think she sees her as a human grandchild.

"Speaking from personal experience, I can honestly say that I have never had problems keeping Chihuahuas in a household where there are children. However, this is because I take sensible precautions.

A lot of the trouble is caused when there is inadequate supervision, especially around very young children. Babies and toddlers have a very strong grip, and can easily hurt a Chi. Likewise, a Chi puppy has surprisingly sharp teeth, and can give a nasty nip quite unintentionally.

"I breed from my Chis, and I will not give a puppy to a household with children under the age of eight, unless the parents assure me that they will supervise their child's contact with the puppy. I also explain how they should go about introducing the child to the puppy.

"The best way is to sit the child on the floor. This way, if the puppy and the child get on well, the puppy can climb on to the child's lap without using his feet, avoiding any painful scratches. Similarly, if the puppy has had enough of being cuddled, and jumps off, he is less likely to hurt himself or the child. For some reason, I have found that very young children have a tendency to believe that Chis can fly! If a Chihuahua is dropped, even from the height of a child's chest, it is a very long way. The golden rule is to never leave young children and dogs – of any breed – alone together."

*Frijole and Spicie love to be part of all the family activities.*

## THE RESIDENT DOG

Chihuahuas are sociable little dogs; they thrive on company, both human and canine. If you already have a dog at home, there should be no problems introducing a Chihuahua puppy, regardless of the breed of your resident dog. It does seem that Chihuahuas get on particularly well with other Chihuahuas, but there have been many examples of friendships with other breeds.

In the early stages, it is important to supervise interactions. A tiny Chihuahua puppy can be frightened by the advances of a bigger dog, even though the intentions may be friendly.

*The sociable Chihuahua is happy to live with other dogs – both big and small.*

- Start off by holding the Chihuahua puppy in your lap, and calling your resident dog over to you.
- Let the older dog sniff the puppy, and give both pup and adult lots of praise.
- Allow the pup on the floor, and let the two dogs meet each other without intervening. In most cases, there will be lots of tail-wagging, and the pup will show he is submissive toward the older dog.

If your resident dog growls, do not rush to pick up the puppy. This will send out all the wrong messages. The dog and puppy must sort out their own relationship, and if you are overprotective of the puppy, the resident dog will feel slighted. Of course, you must use your common sense – if the pup is in any danger of being harmed, you must pick him up.

Make sure you supervise interactions for the first couple of days, and be ready to praise your resident dog when he is friendly toward the puppy. It is also important to set aside some time to spend with your older dog so that he still feels special.

As the puppy gets older, he may seek to become the "top dog" of the house. Again, this is a matter that the two dogs should be left to decide. Interestingly, status, as defined in canine terms, is not a matter of size. There are many examples of a Chihuahua achieving top dog status despite being the smallest dog in the house – even when the Chihuahua is living with a Great Dane!

## ADDING A LITTLE SPICE

Chihuahua breeder Lynn Hunter (Spice Chihuahuas), from Lubbock, Texas, has kept Chihuahuas and German Shepherds together in harmony for several years. Here, she tells the secrets of her success.

"I breed Chihuahuas, and when my two German Shepherds came to live with me and my family, I had 15, so it was vital that all the dogs learned to get along with each other," said Lynn.

"First to join our family was Cinder, a beautiful long-coated Shepherd, aged 14 weeks when she arrived. Unfortunately, I had to rehome Cinder because I developed an allergy to her coat, but before she left, she had made great friends with all my Chis. A year after Cinder's arrival, Delilah joined the family. She was harder to train than Cinder, but with patience, she too became the best of friends with her new canine companions.

"To begin with, I kept the GSDs separate from the Chis, as I wanted to give the Shepherds time to adjust to their new surroundings. I wanted to make sure that introducing the Shepherds to the Chihuahuas did not lead to behavioral problems, so I made sure that the Shepherds were house trained, well socialized, and trained in basic obedience before I introduced them to my Chis.

*German Shepherds Cinder and Delilah relax with Chihuahua Mariah (Spice's Wind 'N' Fire).*

### TAKING CONTROL

"Shepherds are large dogs, and if they were spooked by the Chis, they could easily have hurt them. By leaving the introductions until the Shepherds were slightly older, and more self-disciplined, I gave myself much more control over the introductions.

"I began by introducing my youngest Chis, usually puppies between the ages of 5 to 16 weeks. This was an important part of socialization for my puppies. By introducing them to GSDs while they were still in their first stages of socialization and puppy development, I hoped to ensure that they would mature into confident, well-adjusted adults, totally unfazed by the presence of larger breeds. Young puppies are far more open to new experiences, so they show a lot less fear. In turn, this was great for the Shepherds. It was far easier for them to accept young Chihuahuas, who, because they were not scared, were not at all aggressive.

"I introduced my older Chihuahuas once the Shepherds had matured a little and were comfortable around the younger Chis. Chihuahuas can be guilty of displaying aggressive, terrierlike behavior, and I wanted to make sure that my Shepherds would be able to handle this before I made any introductions. When I eventually did introduce them, everything went smoothly.

# ADDING A LITTLE SPICE

"I only had a few difficult experiences in getting my Chis to mix happily with other breeds. One of these was when my second Shepherd, Delilah, came into season for the first time. One of my male Chihuahuas took a great deal of interest in her, and she took his advances as an intention to play. Without constant supervision, it would have been all too easy for her to have mated with him, or for them to become aggressive with each other. It took nearly a year of behavioral training to overcome the problem.

"I also had a problem with my male Doberman. When my female Chis came into heat, he would become aggressive toward the male Chihuahuas, and it took a lot of training and supervision to overcome this. I would recommend anyone who keeps more than one breed of dog together to make sure that all the dogs are neuteured or spayed, although in my case, that was not possible because I breed my dogs.

"With training, I overcame the problems between my Chis and my Rhodesian, but I wouldn't recommend the combination to anyone else, particularly someone who does not understand canine behavior and who is not experienced at overcoming behavioral problems.

"The golden rule with introducing two very different breeds of dog is constant supervision. Even now, I never allow Delilah to be truly alone with my Chis – I always keep the dogs in sight. However, different breeds can live in harmony, and Delilah and one of my Chis can prove this. Spice's Mocha Latte Te-ya, or Te-ya for short, is the greatest of buddies with Delilah. They are pretty much inseparable, constantly by each other's side. Te-ya was born after Delilah had matured into a fully grown adult, so Delilah accepted her straightaway. However, I don't believe this would have been possible had it not been for Delilah's carefully controlled introductions to my other Chihuahuas when she first arrived."

## BREED TRAITS

"I would also recommend that anyone thinking of adding another breed of dog to a household with a pet Chihuahua should thoroughly research their chosen new breed. For example, I experienced very little difficulty with Chihuahuas and German Shepherds, and my Doberman also lived in harmony with the Chis. However, I also owned a Rhodesian Ridgeback, before I sadly lost him to old age, and he was much harder to control around the Chis. I think this is because Rhodesians were bred to hunt lions. Chihuahuas are so small that they can, occasionally, bring out the prey instinct in dogs that have been bred to hunt.

*You may be surprised at the bond your Chihuahua forms with a dog of another breed. Delilah has "adopted" most of Lynn's Chihuahuas.*

## CATS AND CHIHUAHUAS

There is no reason why a cat and a Chihuahua should not live in harmony, but it is important to get relations off to a good start. A Chihuahua puppy is considerably smaller than a cat, and a frightened feline can inflict a serious injury within seconds if she feels threatened.

- Start off by holding your puppy on your lap, and inviting the cat to come and investigate. An alternative is to confine the puppy in his crate, and allow the cat to come up and sniff. The aim is for the cat to meet the puppy without feeling threatened.
- Do not force the cat to come close to the puppy, and give her lots of reassurance.
- When your pup is looking at the cat, distract

## RULING THE ROOST

For Saffy, a smooth-coated, fawn Chihuahua, it was a matter of sink or swim. Alison Gunson's 12-year-old daughter, Ilona, had always wanted a Chihuahua, and, after two years of persuasion, she finally got her way. Saffy came into the Gunson household, and had to find her feet in a family that included cats, Bulldogs, Hungarian Vizslas, and horses.

"I don't think Saffy had a moment's worry settling in," said Alison. "She is such a big personality, she just took everything in her stride."

When Saffy first arrived as a puppy, there was just one cat, called Granny.

"Granny is used to living with dogs, so she was not about to be put out by a tiny Chihuahua puppy," said Alison. "Because she did not run from the other dogs, Saffy showed very little interest in her."

All that changed when a black and white kitten, called Zorrow, joined the family circle.

"Saffy was absolutely fascinated by the kitten," said Alison. "She was amazed that she had found something smaller than she was.

"Right from the beginning, Saffy and Zorrow would play together – and even though Zorrow is now four times bigger, they are still the best of friends.

"They have a play session every day," said Alison. Their favorite game is chasing each other round and round the rockery. And when they are tired, they will curl up and go to sleep together.

"There was a wonderful moment when Ilona went to sleep on a rug in front of the fire. She was joined by Saffy, Zorrow, a Bulldog, and a Hungarian Vizsla, who all settled down to sleep in a great heap!"

Ilona rides horses, so Saffy has also had to come to terms with larger animals, which must appear like giants from her perspective.

"Saffy is completely unafraid of the horses," said Alison. "In fact, we have to be careful, as she is more than happy to go into the field with them, and we worry about her being trodden on.

"She has been a great addition to our family. She is the only dog that is small enough to pick up and cuddle, and she is always there for us. She will sit with me, watching TV, on the sofa. She will lie under the desk if my husband is working on the computer. And when Ilona goes to bed, she waits on the stairs, and cannot wait to dive under the duvet!"

his attention by offering a treat. Give him lots of praise for responding to you, rather than the cat.

- Repeat this exercise several times a day until the novelty starts to wear off for both cat and Chihuahua.
- The next stage is to allow your pup to meet the cat without being restrained. Be ready with some treats to offer your puppy so that he does not get too focused on the cat, and leave the door open so your cat does not feel trapped. Give lots of praise when your puppy responds to you.
- Repeat this exercise until your cat and your Chihuahua puppy show signs of accepting each other.

For the first few weeks, make sure you are always present when your cat and your puppy are in the same room. If introductions are closely supervised in the early stages, the two animals will learn to accept each other calmly, rather than getting hyped up every time they meet. In time, your cat and your Chihuahua will learn to live together in peace – they may even become good friends.

## CRATE TRAINING

If you have bought a crate or carrier, you will need to get your puppy used to going in it. This should be one of his first lessons.

## Preparing the Crate

- Make the crate look as attractive as possible. Line it with bedding, and put a couple of toys in the crate.

- If you think the crate looks a bit too big for your tiny Chihuahua, you can use a cardboard box so your pup has a cozy bed within his crate.
- Check that the cardboard box has no metal staples. Then cut down the sides of the box, so that it is easy to get in and out of, and line it with bedding.
- A crate can be made more like a den by placing a sheet or a blanket over the top, so that it hangs down the sides of the crate. A pup will feel safe and secure in this environment.

## Settling in the Crate

Puppies are fast learners, and if you spend a little time showing your pup that the crate is a great place to be, he will soon get the idea.

- Start with the crate door open, and tempt your puppy to go in by offering him a treat.
- When the pup is inside, stroke him gently and reassure him.
- Repeat this a couple of times, and then try again in an hour or so.
- It is a good idea to feed your Chihuahua in his crate, because this helps him to build up a favorable association.
- When your pup is happy to go in the crate, close the door, and leave him in there for a few minutes. Make sure you stay in the room, and talk to him to give reassurance.
- Gradually build up the amount of time your

*If a Chihuahua has been trained to use a crate, he will look on it as his own special den.*

pup spends in his crate, and start to leave him alone for short periods.

• Try to choose times when you know your Chihuahua is tired, and then he will be more likely to settle.

If you do not make a big fuss, your puppy will learn to accept being left on his own without feeling anxiety. This is a very important lesson for later life (see Separation Anxiety, page 61), so it is well worth educating your puppy right from the start.

Remember the golden rules of crate training:

• Never leave your Chihuahua confined in his crate for long periods. A crate should be used for short periods when you are going out, or at times when you cannot supervise your pup.
• Never use the crate as a means of punishment. Your puppy should enjoy the quiet times he spends in his "den" – he should not dread being put in there.
• If you leave toys in the crate, make sure they are 100 percent safe.

## HOUSEBREAKING

Housebreaking is an aspect of your puppy's education that you will be eager to get started on. New owners often fear that housebreaking is going to be a major problem that will take months to get right. However, if you follow a few simple rules, you will surprised how quickly your puppy learns to be clean.

Start by allocating an area in the yard that is to be used specifically for toileting purposes. This works on two levels:

• The puppy will learn that this is his toilet area, and will understand why he is being taken outside.
• You will have only one area of the yard to keep clean.

When your puppy first arrives home, take him to his toilet area, and use a command such as "Be clean." When your pup obliges, give him lots of praise.

*If you work hard at housebreaking in the first few weeks, your pup will soon learn to be clean.*

From this point onward, you must take your puppy out at the following times:

- after mealtimes
- after he has woken from a sleep
- after a play session
- every two hours, if he has not already been taken out

When you take your puppy outside, use the same spot in the yard every time, and use the same command. The puppy will soon build up an association, and will understand what is required.

Be lavish in your praise, and then have a little game with your pup before taking him back indoors. If you rush back inside, your puppy may decide to use delaying tactics so that he can stay outside for longer.

Do not make the mistake of letting your puppy out in the yard on his own and hoping that he will relieve himself. In the early stage of training, it is essential that you are in attendance, to instruct your puppy and then to praise him.

You will find that housebreaking is made easier if you are using a crate. A dog is loath to foul his sleeping quarters, and will soon learn to wait until he is let out of his crate before he relieves himself. In the first few weeks, your puppy will struggle to go through the night, so the best plan is to line the front half of his crate with newspaper. The pup will be able to use this and still keep his bed clean.

## When Accidents Happen

It is inevitable that your puppy will make an occasional mistake, but do not fall into the trap of getting angry with him. Nine times out of ten, it will be your fault for failing to take him out at the right time, or failing to spot the signs that he needed to relieve himself.

If you see your puppy circling and sniffing the floor, it is a sure sign that he needs to be taken outside. If you catch him "red-handed," take him outside straightaway, and go to his toilet area. Give him the command – "Be clean" – and then give lots of praise when he responds correctly. A puppy will learn much more quickly if he is rewarded for doing the right thing rather than being punished for making a mistake.

The key is to be vigilant, and to do the thinking for your puppy. Anticipate the times he needs to go out, and then you can build on his success. Do not be too quick to give up this supervisory role. It is better to keep a close check on your puppy until he is so confident that he will ask to go out.

## A BALANCED DIET

The breeder will give you instructions as to how often the puppy should be fed, as well as stipulating the correct quantity. Some breeders may recommend feeding four meals a day; others will suggest that three meals are sufficient. The most important point to remember is that the Chihuahua has a very small stomach, and so he should not be overfed. It is far better to feed small quantities of a high-protein food than to feed too much and allow your puppy to become obese (see page 71).

Some breeders recommend feeding canned food. The Chihuahua puppy has a tiny digestive tract, and this type of food can be easier to cope with. You can buy a small-bite kibble (biscuit) to mix with the meat, but it is a good idea to break the kibble down further, so that your Chihuahua puppy does not have too much of a struggle.

The other option is to feed a dry complete diet, which can be soaked before feeding. The complete diet is specially formulated, and you can be confident that your Chihuahua is receiving the correct balance of nutrients.

There may be a reason why you want to swap from the diet the breeder has been using. You may have a problem with supply, or you may think your Chihuahua puppy may do better on a

*It is best to follow the breeder's recommendations when choosing a diet.*

different diet. If this is the case, do not introduce the change all at once. A puppy has so much to get used to when he first arrives in his new home, that an additional change will inevitably lead to a upset stomach.

Start by introducing a little of the new food at each meal, at the same time reducing the original food. Over a period of a few days, you can make a complete transition.

You will be able to reduce the number of meals as your puppy gets older. Obviously the timing of this will depend on the number of meals you are feeding. As a general guide, your Chihuahua puppy should be on two meals a day by the time he is six months old. However, some owners prefer a routine of feeding three meals a day.

## TEETHING

When your puppy first arrives in his new home, he will have milk teeth. These will be replaced by his adult teeth, which will come through at four to six months of age. During this time, your puppy may have sore gums, so be extra careful when examining his mouth (see Handling, page 40).

As the new teeth push through the gums, your pup will have a great desire to chew – so be ready for him! Make sure you supply your pup with toys that he can chew safely, rather than watching him destroy your home.

While a puppy is teething, his ears may go through an awkward stage and lose their erect carriage. Some Chihuahua pups specialize in having one ear up and one ear down for a brief phase. Do not worry – as soon as your puppy has finished teething, his ears should go back to the correct position.

*Some puppies have a strong urge to chew when they are teething.*

In some cases, weak ears can be strengthened by taping them at the base during puppyhood (don't try this yourself without expert guidance). This problem is most particularly associated with very big ears, which tend to be soft. Most Chihuahuas today develop good, erect ears without assistance.

## HOUSE RULES

A Chihuahua puppy is so small that it is hard to imagine that he will ever get into mischief. Think again! The Chihuahua is a lively, inquisitive little dog, and will be ruling the roost in no time, unless you impose a few house rules.

It is important to decide what you consider to be acceptable behavior and what is out of bounds – and then stick to it. A dog will become confused if you keep changing the rules. For example, you may be happy to allow your Chihuahua to lie on the sofa – but when he has muddy paws you may feel differently.

In this instance, it is best either to teach your puppy that the sofa is *always* off-limits, or to provide some bedding so that he is *always* allowed on the sofa, regardless of how muddy he is.

Consistency is vital in all aspects of dog training, so draw up some house rules, and make sure all members of the family stick to them at all times.

Every household is different, but these are some of the areas you need to consider:

*It is important for a puppy to learn the house rules.*

- Is my Chihuahua allowed on the sofa?
- Is my Chihuahua allowed to sleep on my bed?
- Is my Chihuahua allowed upstairs?
- Is my Chihuahua allowed to beg for food?
- Is my Chihuahua allowed to jump up to greet visitors?

If your dog understands what behavior is appropriate, you will avoid conflict and be well on the way to building up a good human-canine partnership.

## EXERCISE

A Chihuahua puppy is not going to need any more exercise than he gets from playing in the yard. Although a pup should be taken out to be socialized (see below), he does not need exercising in a formal sense until he is six to eight months of age. A Toy puppy is very vulnerable while he is growing, so it is important not to put too much strain on the bones and on the joints.

For information on exercising the adult Chihuahua, see page 71.

## SOCIALIZATION

This is probably the most important part of your puppy's early education – and it has far-reaching effects on how your dog will mature.

A dog has to learn by experience, and the more experiences he is exposed to, the better able he is to cope with adult life. Generally, the Chihuahua is an outgoing, confident dog, but if you stand only a few inches off the ground, the world can be a daunting place.

Some Chihuahuas are more sensitive than others, and if your puppy is the shy, retiring type, you will need to work hard at his socialization, giving lots of praise and encouragement.

### Mean Machines

Start off by accustoming your puppy to all the sights and sounds that you find in a busy home. Household appliances such as the washing machine or the vacuum cleaner may seem innocuous, but a puppy can find them quite alarming.

Try the following routine to help your puppy overcome his fears:

- Sit on the floor next to the washing machine (for example), and encourage your puppy to come toward you. You can encourage him with a toy or a treat.
- When the puppy is focused on playing a game, or eating his treat, switch on the machine, making sure it is set on a gentle cycle.
- Ignore the sound of the machine, and

*If you spend time familiarizing your Chihuahua with all the sights and sounds of a busy household, he will be calm and relaxed in all situations.*

continue playing with the pup. Ideally he will be absorbed in his game and will not be worried by the machine.

- Switch off the machine after a few minutes, and repeat the exercise on a later occasion.
- If your puppy does appear frightened, do not force him to confront the machine. Equally, do not mollycoddle him, or he will think there is a reason to be fearful.
- The best plan is to move some distance from the machine and gradually move closer to it as your pup becomes more confident. This may take a few training sessions.

If you are patient, your puppy will soon learn that machines are part of everyday life. Remember to give lots of praise and reassurance, and to reward with treats, or by playing a game with a favorite toy.

## Strange Sights

We are so used to the world we live in that it is hard to imagine that a man wearing a funny hat could be alarming. Generally, a well-bred puppy should not be unduly nervous, but it will certainly help if you broaden his horizons. This can be done at home, before your puppy has completed his vaccinations.

Invite some friends to come and meet the puppy. This will give him the opportunity to meet people outside his immediate family. Also make sure children come to visit (see page 27).

When your puppy is becoming more confident, you can try a few scenarios that are slightly more challenging. You can

- wear a funny hat,
- put on a pair of sunglasses,
- open an umbrella and leave it on the floor for your puppy to investigate,
- play a musical instrument,
- bang two saucepan lids together.

It doesn't matter what you do. The object of the exercise is to show your puppy that people come in different shapes and guises, but that there is no reason to be frightened. In all instances, encourage your puppy to come up and play, or give him a tasty treat. Make socialization sessions fun, and your puppy will see it all as one big game.

## Handling

A puppy must learn to accept all-over handling.

*Start by gently brushing the coat.*

*Pick up each paw in turn and examine the pads and the nails.*

*Check that the ears are clean.*

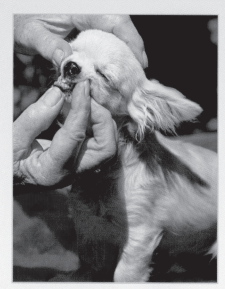

*Open the mouth and look at the teeth.*

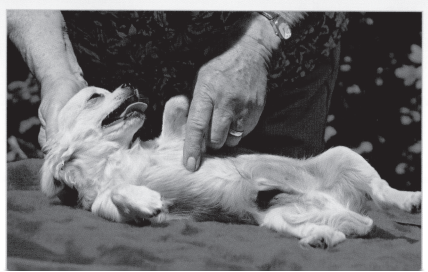

*Lay your pup on his back and tickle his tummy.*

This is important in terms of grooming and routine care (see page 71), and also for the purposes of a veterinary examination (see page 43).

- Start by stroking your puppy and rewarding him with a treat when he sits calmly.
- Some owners prefer to have the puppy on their lap for handling; others use the opportunity to get the puppy used to being on a grooming table.
- You can progress to brushing your puppy's coat with a soft baby brush. This gets the pup used to being groomed (which is particularly important if you have a long-coated Chihuahua), and also to being handled all over. (See Grooming, pages 71–78.)
- Pick up his paws, one by one, and check the nails and the pads. Your puppy's nails will need trimming on a regular basis (see page 77), so he needs to learn to accept having his feet touched without putting up a struggle.
- Look into his ears, and check that they are clean with no evidence of bad odor (see page 76).
- Open his mouth to check his teeth. Your Chihuahua will need to have his teeth cleaned regularly throughout his life, so it is important that your puppy gets used to the attention (see page 75).
- Encourage your puppy to lie on his back – you can usually do this by tickling his tummy.

Reward your puppy at every stage. If he objects, do not force your attentions on him. Be tactful, and if, for example, he objects to having his ears examined, reward him after touching his ear, and then progress in small stages until he accepts the attention.

When you have finished your examination, lift your puppy from the table and have a game with him.

## Car Travel

Your puppy will not be allowed into the outside world until he has completed his full course of inoculations (see Chapter Eight), but while you are waiting, you can get him used to car travel.

Most dogs love traveling in the car, and the Chihuahua is no exception. An outing provides a welcome change of scene – and Chihuahuas love being involved in family activities. It is your job to ensure that your dog travels safely, and is not a nuisance when he is in the car.

*Chihuahuas love a trip out in the car.*

It is strongly recommended that you use a crate or carrier when your Chihuahua is in the car. A dog that is loose can easily be injured if the car has to stop suddenly, and he can also be a distraction to the driver.

If your puppy is used to going in a crate (see page 34), he will be happy to settle in the car. To begin with, he may voice his feelings, but if you ignore him, he will realize that barking does not achieve anything.

Occasionally, a Chihuahua may suffer from car sickness. In most cases, this is a temporary phase, which your dog will quickly grow out of. If your puppy is prone to car sickness, make sure you do not feed him before a trip in the car, and keep journeys short. If the problem persists, consult your veterinarian.

## Visiting the Veterinarian

After your puppy has had a chance to settle into his new home, it is a good idea to make an appointment with the vet so that the pup can be given a general checkup.

It is important that relations with the vet get off to a good start. Dogs are very quick to build up associations – both good and bad. The last thing you want is a dog who connects the vet with pain or discomfort, because you will end up with a very reluctant patient.

The first time you go to the vet, make sure you take plenty of tasty treats. Keep your puppy on your knee, and make sure he is not intimidated by bigger dogs in the waiting room.

If you have chosen a vet who understands Toy dogs (see page 21), he will be tactful in his approach and handling. Be ready to reward your puppy with a treat – though you may well find your vet has his own supply!

The vet will give your puppy an examination, and should also check his heartbeat. You can check when inoculations are due, and you can also discuss worming and flea treatments (see Chapter Eight).

## Puppy Parties

A number of veterinary practices and training clubs run classes specifically for young puppies. In most cases, a puppy is allowed to attend after he has had his first inoculation.

The advantage of these classes is that puppies have the opportunity to mix with each other in a protected environment. This is essential in terms of health safeguards, but it also means that the puppies are meeting on equal footing in terms of age and experience.

This is particularly important for the Chihuahua, who is destined to go through life being dwarfed by fellow canines. If your puppy gets the chance to play with other pups in this type of setup, it will boost his confidence and he will learn the social skills that are essential for canine interactions.

## Out and About

When your puppy has completed his inoculations, you can venture into the outside world. This is a steep learning curve, and you should be careful not to overwhelm your puppy in the early stages.

To begin with, you can carry your puppy, so

that he has the reassurance of being held when he is getting used to a new situation. However, you should not delay lead training (see page 52). If you treat your Chihuahua as a lapdog who cannot stand on his own four feet, he will become exactly that. Be tactful, and try to see the world from your Chihuahua's viewpoint. He may be small, but he still wants to be taken seriously as a dog.

*A well-socialized Chihuahua takes all situations in stride.*

Try the following situations for early socialization:

• Take your Chihuahua to a shopping center, and sit on a bench with your puppy in your lap. This will give your pup the chance to get used to crowds and traffic at a distance.
• Go to the park and find an area where children are playing. Let your Chihuahua watch what is going on and get used to the sound of children at play.
• Visit the local train station or bus station so that your pup can get used to the hustle and bustle of a busy public place. If it is very busy, carry the pup so he doesn't get trampled.
• Find a pet-supply store where dogs are allowed, and do a little shopping.
• Find an opportunity to meet some livestock – chickens, sheep, cattle, or horses. Your Chihuahua needs to accept all living creatures without becoming fearful or barking a protest.

If your Chihuahua is worried by a situation, give gentle reassurance, and distract his attention with a toy or a treat. Do not allow "no-go areas" – avoiding situations because your pup was frightened – or you will find the world becoming a very small place. If your pup is worried, be extra tactful, keeping some distance away from whatever is frightening him, and then gradually build up his confidence with verbal encouragement and rewards.

In most cases, a dog will take the lead from his owner. If you make a huge fuss over your

*Give your pup a good, all-around education, and he will mature into a well-adjusted adult.*

puppy every time he appears a little nervous, you will end up with a neurotic dog. Be confident and positive, and your Chihuahua will learn that there is nothing to be frightened of.

Socialization is a vital part of your puppy's early education, but do not stop the outings when your Chihuahua is full-grown. This is a breed that thrives on variety and human companionship. Even if you are only going to send a letter, your Chihuahua will want to come. It may seem unexciting to you, but as far as your Chihuahua is concerned, it is a trip out, with a good chance of finding something interesting to see or smell!

# CHAPTER FOUR

# TRAINING TARGETS

Owners of Toy dogs are divided on the subject of training. For some, the bonus of having a small dog is that it does not need very much training. A Toy dog is not going to yank your arm off if he pulls on the lead, and he is not going to knock you flying if he jumps up to greet you. But is that a good reason to ignore your dog's brain power?

The Chihuahua is a highly intelligent dog; he is a quick thinker who thrives on the stimulation of having things to do. If you treat him purely as a lapdog, he will be missing out on an important part of his life.

One of the great pleasures of owning a Toy dog is that you can take him almost everywhere you go. However, this is possible only if you have trained him to behave in a civilized manner so that he is never a nuisance. Look on your Chihuahua as an ambassador of the dog world, who can be taken everywhere and is always a credit to you.

## DESCENDED FROM WOLVES

A Toy dog's mind works in exactly the same way as that of a giant breed. Regardless of size or strength, all dogs have a common root. They are descended from the wolf, and over thousands of years they have been domesticated to become companions of man.

The wolf is a pack animal, which means that he lives within a social hierarchy and accepts his status within the pack. The Chihuahua may not appear very wolflike, but he retains an instinctive understanding of pack behavior. This means that he will be looking for leadership, and will be ready to abide by the rules that are set within his own community.

Do not fear that you are going to have to take on the role of a menacing pack leader, barking orders at your little Chihuahua. This is the equivalent of taking a sledgehammer to crack a nut. Your task is to provide a clear set of rules that your Chihuahua will be happy to abide by. Your leadership should always be kind and

*A Toy dog needs training just as much as a larger breed.*

consistent, backed up with reward and praise, so that your Chihuahua is always motivated to do as you ask.

## MOTIVATION

Having established that the Chihuahua is prepared to accept leadership, we now need to encourage him to be an eager and willing pupil. We are all capable of learning in a dull, unstimulating environment. But our response is likely to be slow and halfhearted. Imagine how much brighter we would be if the teacher was fired with enthusiasm and we knew we were working for something we really wanted.

It is exactly the same for a dog that is being trained. He will do as he is told, but unless he has the motivation, he will put in minimal effort.

There are many ways you can motivate a dog; it is a question of knowing your pet and finding out how his mind works. Some dogs will do anything for a tasty treat; others will prefer a game with a favorite toy. Experiment with your Chihuahua, and monitor his responses. He may be eager to work for a treat, but if you find an extra-special treat, such as a piece of cheese or a bit of cooked liver, you may find that your Chihuahua is ready to pull out all the stops!

## COUNTING CALORIES

It is essential to give your Chihuahua a balanced diet and to guard against obesity (see page 71). If you are training with treats, figure out how much food you are giving your dog, and then deduct it from his regular rations.

## CLICKER TRAINING

Clicker training is a system of reward-based training that was first pioneered by Karen Pryor when she was working with dolphins. It has since been adapted, and is proving hugely successful with a wide range of animals. Dogs, with their high level of intelligence and willingness to please, are ideal candidates.

The clicker is a small box, fitted with a metal tongue that makes a "click" when it is pressed. The handler uses the "click" to mark good behavior; it is a signal that says, "Yes, this is what I want." The click is followed by giving a reward. This is usually in the form of a treat, but it can be a game with a toy, or simply verbal praise and stroking.

The big advantage of this form of training is

that the dog learns to work for his treats. He knows he has to get his owner to "click" before he gets a reward. Dogs catch on to this very quickly, and love the stimulation and reward of this type of training.

## DO NOT FORGET...

Whatever training method you use, and whatever reward you choose, do not forget to give verbal and physical praise. Your Chihuahua is trying to please you: if he succeeds, he should be given lavish verbal praise and a cuddle.

Tone of voice is all-important when you are training a dog. Remember, he does not understand the meaning of the words you are using; your tone of voice tells him whether he is responding correctly. Make sure you sound bright and enthusiastic when you are teaching your dog, and be ready to go over the top with the praise when he gets it right!

## BASIC TRAINING

It is a good plan to work out which exercises you want to teach, and the order you are going to attempt them in. Some exercises follow on as a natural progression; others, such as the retrieve, are optional extras.

### Sit

This is the simplest exercise to teach, and you can start working on it as soon as your puppy has settled into his new home.

- Arm yourself with a treat, and hold it just above the puppy's head.

*Use a treat to lure your puppy into the Sit position.*

- As the puppy looks up, he will naturally go into the Sit position. This may take a few moments, but if you persevere, your pup will run out of available options.
- If you are using a clicker, click the moment your pup starts to go into position.

- Reward with praise and a treat.
- Repeat the exercise a few times until your pup understands what you want. Be lavish in your praise when your Chihuahua responds correctly.
- You can continue the exercise at mealtimes by holding the food bowl just above your puppy's head, and waiting for him to sit before you put it down.
- When you are confident that your puppy understands the exercise, introduce the command "Sit" as soon as he goes into position. In time, he will learn to associate the word with the reaction, and will respond as soon as you give the command.

### Down

The Down is an extension of the Sit, and can be taught as soon as your pup has mastered this first exercise.

- Start with your pup in the Sit, and show him that you have a treat in your hand.
- Then, close your fist around the treat and lower your hand toward the ground.
- The pup will follow the treat, and, in his efforts to get at it, will lower himself to the ground.
- Some pups try all sorts of tricks to get at the treat, but if you keep your fist closed, he will eventually oblige.
- As soon as your pup starts to lower himself into position, click and reward.
- Repeat the exercise until your pup understands what is required, always remembering to give him lots of praise.
- Introduce the command "Down," and gradually increase the time your pup stays in position before rewarding him. With practice, he will respond to the verbal command without being lured into position.

*Lower the treat and your pup will follow it, going into the Down position. Gently praise your pup and reward him with the treat.*

*Hold the treat out to encourage the puppy to stand.*

### Stand

The Stand is not essential for the pet owner, but if you plan to show your Chihuahua (see Chapter Seven: Seeking Perfection), it is a must. In fact, many exhibitors do not teach the Sit, as this is taboo in the show ring.

- Use a treat and hold it out for your puppy so that he can reach it comfortably while he is standing on all four feet.
- Click and reward.
- Repeat the exercise, waiting a little longer each time before giving the reward.
- Introduce the command "Stand," drawing it out "St—and," to encourage your dog to stay in position.

### Come

The Come command is easy to teach while your pup is young, and, if you build up a good response, it will certainly pay dividends in adult life. The Chihuahua is very quick on his feet, and if your dog takes off, you will find there is little hope of catching him!

- When your pup first arrives home, he will follow you everywhere. Capitalize on this by using his name and giving him lots of praise when he comes running up to you.
- If you are using a clicker, click when your pup comes up to you, and reward with a game or a treat.
- When your pup is running in enthusiastically, use his name and the command "Come." Reward and give lots of praise.
- You can make the exercise a little more formal by asking someone to hold on to your pup and then release him when you give the command to come.
- If you get really ambitious, you can ask your pup to sit when he comes to you.

*Give lots of encouragement, so that your puppy wants to come to you.*

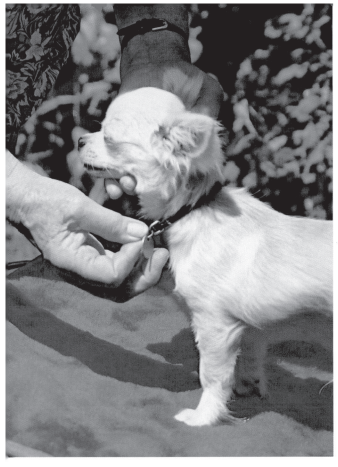

*The puppy must get used to wearing a collar.*

- To begin with, your pup will scratch at the collar and be irritated by it. Distract his attention by playing a game or giving a treat.
- Leave the collar on for a few minutes, and then remove it.
- You can try putting on the collar just prior to giving a meal so that your puppy has a ready means of distraction.
- Gradually increase the amount of time you leave the collar on, until your pup ignores it completely.
- The next step is to attach the lead. To begin with, allow the lead to trail, making sure it does not get snarled up.
- Then, pick up the end of the lead and follow your pup wherever he goes. When he is

Always try to sound exciting when you give the "Come" command. Your puppy should *want* to come to you, knowing he will be greeted with lots of praise and a tasty treat as an added bonus.

### Lead Training

You can work on lead training while you are waiting for your pup to complete his inoculations. Then, when he is ready to venture outside, he will be reasonably proficient on the lead.

- Start by fastening the collar around your puppy's neck. The collar should be lightweight, and should be fastened so that you can slip two fingers underneath it.

*Use a toy or a treat so that the pup learns to follow you on the lead.*

walking happily, click and stop to give a treat.

- Your puppy must now learn to walk with you, rather than choosing his own route.
- It may help if you use a toy to encourage your pup forward, or he may respond better to a treat.
- When you have achieved a few paces of good work, click and reward.
- If your pup lags behind, stop and call him to your side, and then set off again, using lots of verbal encouragement.
- If your pup tries to surge ahead, stop and call him to your side. Set off again, this time trying to keep the pup's attention focused on you, rather than on what lies ahead.
- Be patient, and even if you have achieved just a few paces of walking together, stop and reward.
- Introduce the command "Heel" when you are certain your pup understands what is required.

Practice makes perfect, and there are no shortcuts to lead training. Remember to praise your pup when he is walking nicely on a loose lead. You can use verbal praise or click him to mark the fact that he is doing what you want. You can then stop and reward your pup with a treat or a game.

Make sure you give the "Heel" command only when your pup is in the correct position.

All too often, lead training goes wrong because the puppy is constantly being told that he is doing the wrong thing, rather than being praised when he is responding correctly.

## Stay

The Stay is a useful exercise and can be used in a variety of different situations. It follows naturally from lead training, as your chances of success are vastly improved if you are working with your Chihuahua on a lead.

Make sure you teach the Stay as a separate unit to avoid confusion with the Come exercise.

- Your pup can be taught to stay in the Sit, Stand, or Down. Eventually, you will be able to work with your Chihuahua in all three positions, but it is best to concentrate on just one to begin with.
- Put your pup on the lead, and put him in the position you have chosen.

*Build up the Stay exercise in easy stages.*

- Step one pace to the side of your pup, and use a hand signal (palm facing toward your pup) to show he must stay in position.
- Step back to your pup's side, click, and praise.
- Repeat the exercise, introducing the command "Stay" when you are confident that your pup has got the right idea.
- If your pup attempts to get up to join you, just put him back in position and try again.
- Try stepping one pace in front of your pup, and then one pace to the rear, so that he learns to Stay regardless of where you are positioned.
- Gradually increase the distance you leave your puppy. Do not rush this stage, or you will upset your pup, and he will start to feel concerned about being left.
- When you return to your pup's side, click and praise him quietly. It is useful to have a release word, such as "OK," so that your pup knows when he is allowed to break position. He can then be rewarded with lots of fuss and a game.

## Retrieve

It is not necessary to teach your Chihuahua to retrieve, but it is a fun game that he will enjoy playing.

- Start by getting your puppy interested in a toy. It can be anything you or your puppy likes, as long as it is easy to pick up and is not too heavy to carry.
- Play a game of tug, and then a game of hide-and-seek so that your pup becomes focused on his toy.

- Then throw the toy a short distance. If your pup goes to pick it up, click and give lots of praise.
- If your pup loses interest, keep on playing with the toy, and try again in a few moments. Click and reward your pup if he approaches the toy.
- Build up this exercise in easy stages, until your puppy is picking up the toy. At this stage you can introduce a command, such as "Hold."
- The next part of the exercise is to teach your pup to bring his retrieve toy back to you.
- When your pup picks up the toy, call his name and give the command "Come." If you are very lucky, your pup will come running toward you, carrying his toy. If this happens, you can give lavish praise.

However, it is more likely that the pup will try to run off with his toy, or drop it on his way back to you. There are a couple of ways of counteracting this.

### First Method

Arm yourself with a toy. When you call your pup, he will, ideally, come running in to see what you have. Click and reward, and then exchange toys with him. This teaches him that coming back to you does not signal the end of the game, so he will be less likely to run off with his "trophy."

### Second Method

If your pup keeps running off, you can take control of his retrieve toy by tying it on the

## THE RETRIEVE

*This Chihuahua has been taught to do a formal retrieve with his dumbbell, but if you feel this is a bit ambitious, you can do a fun retrieve with a toy.*

*Command your dog to "Wait."*

*Throw the dumbbell.*

*The dog runs out to pick up his dumbbell.*

*He runs back, holding the dumbbell.*

*He comes in close to present the dumbbell.*

end of a length of cord. Throw the toy, and let your pup run out to fetch it. Then, when he has the toy, you can call him, gently guiding the toy in your direction. When your pup comes to you, click, and give him lots of praise and a treat. He will soon learn that it is more rewarding to come back to you than to run off on his own.

### Fun Tricks

There are lots of tricks you can teach your Chihuahua after he has mastered the basic exercises. You can train him to sit up and beg, shake hands, or roll over. It does not matter what the exercise is; you are providing your Chihuahua with mental stimulation, plus the bonus of interacting with his owner.

### TRAINING CLUB

If you enroll in a training class, you will have an excellent means of socializing your Chihuahua as well as getting help and advice with his training. However, it is important to do your homework and find a club that is suitable for both you and your dog.

Go to a class without your Chihuahua and check out the following points:

• **Does the club have classes for dogs that are training at different levels?** Ideally, the club will run a number of classes to suit different levels of experience and expertise. However, if you live in a small community, there may be enough members for only one class. This does not have to be a drawback as long as

the class is well run and the tinies are not intimidated by bigger dogs.

• **Do the instructors use positive methods of training, which are based on reward?** This is by far the most effective way to train, and you do not want to be part of a club that believes in yanking dogs on the lead as a means of "correcting" behavior.

• **Does the club use clicker training?** Again, this is not essential, but it should be considered a bonus. Experienced clicker trainers can help you improve your timing so that you and your dog get the maximum benefit from this method of training.

• **Do the instructors have experience in training Toy dogs?** This is important, as you need an instructor who has realistic expectations of your Chihuahua's capabilities.

• **Do they have classes for training show dogs?** Some clubs are devoted to conformation handling, specializing in training pedigree dogs for the ring. Other clubs may allocate a class for this purpose. Obviously, this is of interest only if you plan to show your Chihuahua (see Chapter Seven: Seeking Perfection).

Many owners work hard at training, and then give up once their dog is full-grown. Training should be seen as a continuous business that carries on throughout your dog's life.

Interacting with your dog is a richly rewarding experience – and your Chihuahua will enjoy every minute of the time that you have allocated especially for him.

## TROUBLESHOOTING

Despite all the effort you put into your Chihuahua's training, sometimes things go wrong. It may be that your dog is naturally a bit pushy and is trying to rule the roost, or you may have spoiled him a little too much and given him an inflated idea of himself.

Do not despair: the Chihuahua is a bright little dog, and if you work at breaking bad habits, you will generally succeed.

Fortunately, cases where a Chihuahua misbehaves because he has poor temperament are very rare.

*If your Chihuahua develops behavioral problems, you must find out what has gone wrong.*

## THE SPOILED CHIHUAHUA

The most common cause of Chihuahua problems are the owners who cannot resist spoiling their pet. This generally stems from feeling overprotective toward the tiny Chihuahua, and failing to treat him like a proper dog. If a big dog behaves badly, we are forced to do something about it. If a Chihuahua misbehaves, nine times out of ten, the owner will pick him up to halt the behavior. This is a short-term solution, and you are only storing up trouble for the future.

If a dog (of any breed) is allowed to get the upper hand, he will be quick to take advantage. The relationship between dog and owner will become unbalanced – and misery will result. The dog will continually try to push back the boundaries to show he can do as he pleases. This may take the form of

- flouting house rules by jumping on to furniture that is out of bounds,
- excessive barking,
- growling if anyone comes near his bed or tries to move him from the place he has chosen to sleep,
- becoming possessive over his food bowl or his toys.

These behaviors may seem wide-ranging, but they have a common thread. The Chihuahua has lost respect for his owner.

If you are worried that this has happened, or you fear the relationship is deteriorating, you must take immediate action. A dog is swift to learn bad habits, and once these become established, they are increasingly difficult to break.

## REESTABLISHING LEADERSHIP

The Chihuahua is a clever little dog, and if you work on a retraining program, he will soon realize the game is up and you are back in charge.

You can reassert your authority in the following ways:

### Food Issues

- Always feed your Chihuahua after the family has eaten, so that he understands he is an inferior member of the family pack.

- Do not feed treats from the table when you are eating, and give food treats only as a reward for good behavior.
- If your Chihuahua is possessive about his food bowl, drop in a few treats while he is eating so that he will learn to welcome the interference.
- Progress to taking the bowl away for a few seconds and then allowing your dog to continue eating. In this way, your Chihuahua will learn that you must be respected as the provider of his food.

### House Rules

- Decide where your dog is allowed to go (the sofa, the armchair, and so on), and what is off-limits.

*Drop some treats into the food bowl, so that your Chihuahua learns not to resent your interference.*

- Be 100 percent consistent, and stop your Chihuahua every time he attempts to go somewhere that is forbidden. This does not have to result in a confrontation. Tell him "No" firmly if he tries to jump on the sofa, and then distract his attention by offering him a treat or a game with a toy.
- You can then take your Chihuahua to his bed (or the chair that he is allowed on), and ask him to sit or to lie down. Reward your Chihuahua with lots of praise – even if he stays in position for only a few moments. In time, he will learn it is more rewarding to go to his own bed than to break house rules.

### GUARDING

- If your Chihuahua growls when you invade his personal space by coming too close to his bed, you must show that you "own" his bed and that he is allowed to use it only when you say so.
- When your Chihuahua is in his bed, offer him a treat and stroke him while he is eating it. This will build up a good association so that your Chihuahua learns to welcome your coming up to his bed.
- Next, offer your Chihuahua a treat so that he has to come out of his bed to get it. With some dogs, offering a game with a toy may be more effective.
- After giving the treat, or playing with a toy, tell your Chihuahua to go back to bed, and then praise him.
- Repeat the above exercises a number of times each day, and your Chihuahua will learn that

*A dog may become possessive about his bed or a favorite toy.*

you are in control of his bed, and that it is not a no-go area.

### Play Sessions

- If your Chihuahua has started to become possessive about his toys, he must be retrained so that he understands that the toys belong to you, and that he can play with them only when you say so.
- Keep your Chihuahua's toys to one side so that he does not have free access to them.
- Introduce a toy during a play session, and allow your Chihuahua to take hold of it. Then, offer him a treat (or another toy) so that he will happily make an exchange. Repeat this several times.
- At the end of the play session, put all the toys away.
- Work on a few basic training exercises with your Chihuahua, and let him play with a toy

as his reward. Gradually, your dog will realize that you control the toys, and that his good behavior results in a game with a toy.

## EXCESSIVE BARKING

- An assertive Chihuahua may like the sound of his voice, and will decide that barking is a good way of getting attention. This is completely different from the Chihuahua who barks when he is left on his own and is experiencing separation anxiety (see page 61).
- If your Chihuahua barks for attention, do not resort to shouting at him, telling him to be quiet. As far as your dog is concerned, he is

*Barking can quickly develop into a bad habit.*

getting what he wants – attention.

- Ignore your Chihuahua when he is barking, and, as soon as he is quiet, distract his attention with a toy or a treat. Make sure you do not give the treat or the toy when the dog is barking, or he will think his inappropriate behavior is being rewarded.
- If you are really struggling, you can use a deterrent that will stop your Chihuahua in midbark. Use a water pistol, and give your Chihuahua a quick squirt of water when he is barking.
- Your dog will be momentarily surprised, which will silence him. You can then introduce a toy or a treat and reward him while he is quiet. The advantage of this tactic is that the Chihuahua does not associate the squirt of water with you, but he is quick to realize that something unpleasant happens when he barks.

### Mental Stimulation

- All too often, a bored Chihuahua becomes a badly behaved Chihuahua, so work at keeping your dog's mind occupied.
- Break up the day with outings in the car, take your dog to the local park, or go window shopping. This will provide variety in your Chihuahua's life.
- Play a game with your Chihuahua, such as throwing his favorite toy for him to retrieve.
- Work on basic training exercises, and introduce some fun tricks so your Chihuahua can enjoy showing off.
- Spend some time grooming your Chihuahua.

*A Chihuahua may become so reliant on his owner that he feels he cannot cope on his own.*

He will benefit from the quality time he is spending with you, as well as from looking his best.

## SEPARATION ANXIETY

The Chihuahua thrives on human companionship, and if your dog had his way, he would be with you every second of the day. This is one of the most endearing traits of the Chihuahua's character, but unfortunately, it can cause problems. No matter how devoted an owner you are, you cannot be at your Chihuahua's side every minute of the day and night, and he must learn to cope when he is left alone.

The dog who becomes too dependent on his owner will experience separation anxiety when he is home alone, and this can be expressed in a number of different ways:

- The dog may become destructive.
- He may bark or whine continuously when he is left.
- His housebreaking may lapse.

There is no need for any of these problems to arise if you train your Chihuahua to accept periods on his own. Start from the moment you get your Chihuahua, by teaching him to settle in his crate (see page 34).

If this lesson is learned at an early stage, the puppy will realize that there is no need to panic when he is left alone, because you always come back. The best plan is to build up the amount of time your puppy spends on his own in easy stages, so that he becomes increasingly confident and self-reliant.

If you have failed to train your puppy to be on his own, and your adult Chihuahua is experiencing separation anxiety, you must attempt to resolve the situation. It is not kind to allow your Chihuahua to become so focused on you that he cannot cope on his own.

### Teaching Self-reliance

- Invest in a crate or a carrier, so that you know your Chihuahua has a safe, secure place where he can be left alone. The added advantage is that a Chihuahua who is confined in a crate cannot be destructive. It will also help if your Chihuahua's housebreaking lapses when he is left alone, because he will be far less likely to foul his own sleeping quarters.

- Accustom your Chihuahua to going into his crate (see page 34). To begin with, stay in the same room, gradually building up the amount of time your Chihuahua is in his crate.

- It is also a good idea to buy a solid child gate (not an accordian-style one) and use it between two linking rooms. Leave your Chihuahua in one room while you are in the other. In this way, your Chihuahua can still see and hear you, even though he has been left on his own.

- When you go out, leave some toys in the crate so your Chihuahua has something to occupy himself with. The best type are boredom-busters – toys that are designed for secreting treats. The dog can smell the food, and he has to figure out a way of getting it out. This will keep the average Chihuahua fully occupied!

- Make a few mock departures, putting on your coat and jangling the car keys. Leave your Chihuahua for a few minutes, and then return. Your Chihuahua will learn that the signs of departure are not a cause for alarm.

- When you leave the house, do not make a big fuss over your Chihuahua. If you are calm, your Chihuahua will not become hyped up with anxiety.

*A boredom-busting toy will keep your dog occupied while you are away.*

*Chihuahuas thrive on company – human and canine – and getting another dog (or dogs!) can help to overcome separation anxiety.*

• When you return, resist the temptation of rushing to release your Chihuahua. Leave him for a few minutes, and then go to him and praise him – without going over the top.

Separation anxiety can grow into a big problem, and once a dog becomes anxious, it takes time to build up his confidence and self-reliance.

However, if you are patient, and work on the program outlined above, you will get there in the end.

**SUMMING UP**

If you are not making progress with any of the problems outlined above, do not delay in seeking the help of a professional animal behaviorist. You will probably find that your vet can recommend someone suitable.

# CHAPTER FIVE

# CARING FOR YOUR CHIHUAHUA

**A**s your Chihuahua passes out of puppyhood, his needs will change, and you will need to adopt a routine of care and management that will suit the adult dog.

However, there is an in-between period of adolescence, when you may detect some physical and temperamental changes in your Chihuahua.

## COPING WITH ADOLESCENCE

In the human world, parents dread their children's adolescence, which can be a time of strife and difficulty as teenagers come to terms with their increased maturity.

Animals go through a similar adolescent period, and in some breeds of dog, this can be nearly as challenging!

We are fortunate that Chihuahuas seem to suffer from few adolescent hang-ups, and in many cases, owners are hardly aware of the transition into adulthood.

## THE MALE

It is generally thought that Toy dogs mature more quickly than the larger breeds, but this is not necessarily the case with the Chihuahua. A male will not be fully mature until he is around 18 months of age, and his adolescent or "junior" phase is generally around 12–18 months.

At this time, a male Chihuahua may not look his best. He has lost his early bloom, and is at an untidy, slightly gangly stage, caught between puppyhood and adulthood. This is of little consequence to the pet owner, but it can be a nervous time if you are planning to show your Chihuahua.

Temperamentally, the adolescent male may show few changes in behavior. He may mess around a little, and be a bit slower to respond to you, but he is unlikely to be confrontational. Try to be patient with your Chihuahua at this time, and give lots of praise and reward when he responds correctly.

If you are not planning to show your

Chihuahua or use him for breeding, neutering is a sensible option. However, it is important to wait until the dog is fully mature – around 18 months of age – before allowing him to be castrated. If the operation is performed too early, the dog is in a period of suspended development, and this may have an effect on his temperament.

The advantage of neutering is that your Chihuahua will not be on the lookout for bitches in season every time you go out, and he will not feel the need to mark his territory (which he does by cocking his leg) quite so zealously.

*The implications of neutering should be discussed with your vet.*

It has been noted that the long-coated Chihuahua grows a more profuse coat after castration, which can be viewed as a bonus, depending on your enthusiasm for grooming! The other possible side effect is obesity. A castrated dog tends to put on weight more easily, and this must be safeguarded against (see page 71).

In terms of health, a castrated dog will be less likely to suffer prostate disorders, and the risk of testicular cancer is eliminated.

## THE FEMALE

A female Chihuahua is sexually mature when she has had her first season. The timing of this may vary dramatically between individuals: some may have their first season at around eight months, others as old as 15 months.

Despite the major hormonal changes taking place, the female Chihuahua seems to float through adolescence, and rarely gives cause for concern. She is less likely to go through an "ugly duckling" phase than the male, and she will generally continue to be her usual sweet and sunny self.

In most breeds, neutering is recommended for females that are not to be used for breeding, but this is not always the case with Chihuahuas. Compared with castration in the male, spaying in the female is a much more serious operation, and the implications of this should be considered. The tiny Chihuahua is very vulnerable under anesthetic, so there is risk involved. Research has shown that there are health benefits involved with spaying, such as a reduced risk of mammary tumors, and a lower incidence of pyometra (a life-threatening womb infection). However, this must be considered alongside the side effects of obesity and urinary incontinence, which may occur in the spayed female.

This is an important decision to make, and it would be wise to discuss the pros and cons with your vet before taking action.

## LIVING WITH A RESCUED DOG

It is easy to think that if you take on an adult dog, you will be relieved of the trouble of training and socializing your Chihuahua. However, this is rarely the case. An older dog will take some time to adapt to a new home, particularly if he has come from a rescue shelter.

Unfortunately, there are a number of adult Chihuahuas who end up in rescue shelters and are in need of a good home. The majority of dogs find themselves in this situation through no fault of their own. It could be that an elderly owner has died or can no longer look after a dog. In some cases, marital breakup means that the dog no longer has a home, or occasionally a couple have children – and the dog becomes surplus to requirements.

Sometimes the reason is much more straightforward, such as when a breeder wants to find a home for a retired show dog who will benefit from being placed in a loving home, rather than being in a kennel setup.

Regardless of the dog's background, rehoming requires a special kind of dedication. In most

*Sadly, there are a number of Chihuahuas who need rehoming, often through no fault of their own.*

cases, the dog will be disoriented because of the trauma of leaving his home. It takes time for an adult to find his feet in a new environment, and even longer for him to build up a sense of trust with his new owners. However, if you are prepared to take on the challenge, the rewards can be great.

Sylvia Fresson, the UK coordinator for the British Chihuahua Club's rescue service, is the first to say that rehoming a Chihuahua demands commitment, and she has devised a system to ensure, as far as is possible, that the homes that are found will prove to be suitable.

"When people inquire about rehoming a Chihuahua, we send out an application form, which is based on the form used at the UK's Battersea Dogs' Home," she said. "We have found that this gets rid of the time-wasters. We then keep the application on file, and when a dog comes in for rehoming, we look at all the applications and try to find the most suitable home.

"The next stage is for one of our home-checkers to go and check the home. If they give the go-ahead, we are then ready to place the dog."

The most common problems that new owners have to deal with are housebreaking and lack of socialization.

"This is usually the result of a dog that has been taken on by someone who is getting on in years," said Sylvia. "Often, they have not been able to socialize the dog properly, and they have simply overlooked the problem of house training. However, we find that, given time and

*Taking on a rescued dog demands a special commitment.*

understanding, most dogs can be reeducated."

"If we have a Chihuahua who has more serious behavioral problems, such as extreme nervousness, we would place him in a foster home with one of our more experienced carers. We find that the problems are often a result of bad treatment, or the dog has simply not been understood. If we are careful with rehoming, these dogs can overcome their problems and become much-loved pets."

## HOLLY AND IVY

The phone rang one bleak, dark December afternoon, not long before Christmas. It was the kennels, phoning to ask whether we had any reports of a Chihuahua being stolen. A Chihuahua and a Yorkshire Terrier had been found abandoned and tied to railings, and were subsequently taken by the dog warden to the local authority dog pound.

"This local authority has a policy whereby stray dogs are kept for the minimum required period of seven days, allowing time for them to be claimed by their owners. After this period, they are destroyed.

"Fortunately, the lady who rang me owns a nearby boarding kennels and also plays a great part in rescuing and rehoming dogs. She would periodically visit the dog pound and rehome as many of the 'death row' inhabitants as possible. It was here that she found the Chihuahua and the Yorkie, and, as it was just before Christmas, christened them Holly (Chi) and Ivy (Yorkie). They were in very good condition, which prompted her to think that they might have been stolen or abandoned.

"I checked my list of applicants wanting Chihuahuas, and found Marilyn and Jackie, who traveled up the very next day to adopt the two girls. Marilyn continues the story…"

"We arrived at the rescue center and two little dogs were brought from the kennels to meet us. It was a cold day, and they were wearing coats, knitted by friends of the rescue center, to keep them warm.

"After they were microchipped and booked out, we were asked if we wanted to take them home in the woolly coats and post them back later. As our car was heated, and the fleecy blanket for the dogs was already installed on the back seat, we declined.

### MAKING A DIFFERENCE

"On the way home, we visited a pet store. New collars, leads, bowls, and coats were acquired, as well as baskets (one for home and one for my office). There was no need for dog food – some chicken with rice and boiled vegetables was on the menu that day.

"Holly the Chihuahua was boss right from the start – she even scares my sister's two Staffordshire Bull Terriers! Ivy is still very anxious, and doesn't like her routine changed, but she has the most loving, sweet nature. Holly is quite confident that everyone loves her (which is true). She has her favorites among the staff at work – and sits on their laps to be petted.

"We are so pleased to have been able to make a difference to these two dear little dogs."

*Holly (left) and Ivy were given a second chance.*

## CARING FOR THE ADULT CHIHUAHUA

### ADULT DIET

By this stage you will have discovered the diet that suits your Chihuahua. Some food manufacturers have a puppy diet, and then progress to an adult maintenance diet, and it is best to follow the recommended guidelines.

The adult Chihuahua is generally fed two meals a day. It is important not to overburden a small stomach, so it is preferable to divide the rations rather than feed one big meal. You may find that your Chihuahua needs slightly more food in the winter. A small dog loses body heat more rapidly than a larger animal, so he will need a little extra food to maintain body temperature and energy levels.

*The adult Chihuahua will need two meals a day.*

### Finicky Feeders

Chihuahuas seem to come in two varieties: the greedy little dog who will eat everything you put down, and the reluctant feeder who has to be tempted to eat. In most cases, dogs that live together tend to eat well, as they know that if they leave anything, they risk losing it.

The lone Chihuahua can afford to play with his food, and may become finicky if you keep changing his diet in a bid to make him eat more.

If you have a fussy feeder, the best plan is to add a tasty treat to his food. This can be a small slice of cooked chicken, a little piece of sausage, or some grated cheese. The enticing smell of the treat will usually tempt a Chihuahua, and ideally, he will keep going to eat the rest of his meal.

### Bones and Chews

It is important to try to keep your Chihuahua's teeth clean, particularly if you are feeding a soft diet. Regular teeth-brushing is essential (see page 75), but providing a bone, a chew, or a hard biscuit will also help.

Nylon bones and dental chews are good for gnawing, and your Chihuahua will also enjoy a small marrow bone. If you keep more than one dog, you should give a bone or a chew only when the dogs are separated; otherwise quarrels may break out.

In all situations, you should ensure that your Chihuahua is always supervised if he has a bone or a chew.

*The Chihuahua does not need a lot of exercise, but he appreciates variety and mental stimulation.*

### Dangers of Obesity

The Chihuahua is a lively little dog, who should move swiftly and energetically. However, the combination of feeding too much and exercising too little can often lead to obesity. It is no kindness to overindulge a tiny dog, who will be quick to put on weight. The result is a plump dog who finds it difficult to move and therefore starts to lose interest in life.

The repercussions on health are far-reaching. The overweight Chihuahua is far more likely to suffer from heart disease, diabetes, and other related problems. This is a long-lived breed, but an obese Chihuahua is highly unlikely to live to old age.

Resist those pleading eyes, and remember that you are responsible for your dog's health and well-being. If you want to give the occasional treat (particularly if you are training your Chihuahua), make sure you deduct the treats from the daily ration you are feeding.

### EXERCISE

The Chihuahua is a wonderfully adaptable dog, and this is particularly true when it comes to exercise. Once he is full-grown, your Chihuahua will enjoy as much exercise as you give him. However, he will also be happy playing in the yard, just rushing around investigating everything that is going on.

Some Chihuahuas love going for walks, and it is surprising how well they keep up with the pace. A fit Chihuahua will be more than happy to keep you company on a five-mile trek.

If you are unable to provide this sort of exercise, your Chihuahua will keep busy in the house and yard. It is a good idea to introduce some play sessions, such as retrieving a toy (see page 54), so the Chihuahua keeps active and also benefits from some mental stimulation.

### GROOMING

The Chihuahua is a fairly low-maintenance

breed compared with many Toy dogs that have long, luxuriant coats. However, grooming should never be looked on as a chore. It is a time to interact with your Chihuahua, and to give him the individual attention on which he thrives.

It is also an excellent way of keeping a check on your Chihuahua's general health and well-being. If you allocate just 10 minutes every day to brushing your dog, watching out for any unusual lumps, bumps, or cuts, you will detect any sign of trouble at an early stage. If you have a thorough knowledge of your Chihuahua, you will be quick to spot anything out of the ordinary – and this could prove vital in making an early diagnosis.

It is also important to keep a lookout for external parasites, such as fleas and ticks (see Chapter Eight: Health Care).

Most Chihuahuas love being groomed, and will positively look forward to this special part of their day.

## Smooth Coat

The smooth coat is obviously easier to care for, but your Chihuahua will still benefit from regular grooming sessions.

The smooth coat should be close-fitting and glossy. The tail is slightly more furry – it is often described as a beaver tail. The smooth coat may have a small ruff on the neck, and there may also be an undercoat.

Regular grooming with a slicker brush will keep the coat in order. If you have accustomed your Chihuahua to standing on a table, this will make the task much easier. The workload increases when the coat is shedding, which it does in dramatic fashion. Surprisingly, the smooth-coated Chihuahua sheds a prodigious amount of hair. This may take place over a period of weeks, or it may shed more quickly.

During this time, grooming with a small pin brush will help loosen the dead hair and speed up the shedding process. A rubber brush also helps with shedding.

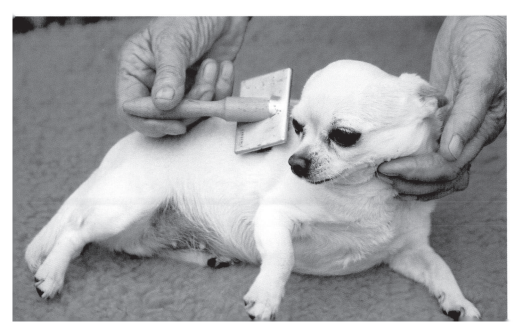

*A small pin brush is useful when the smooth coat is shedding.*

# GROOMING A LONG-COATED CHIHUAHUA

*Start by working through the coat with a bristle brush.*

*You will need to groom the undercarriage.*

*Lift each paw in turn, and groom the feathering on the leg.*

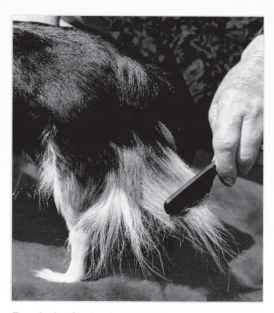

*Brush the feathering, and then use a comb to ensure it is free of tangles.*

## Long Coat

The adult coat of the long-coated Chihuahua usually comes through at around nine months. Typically, the coat should be soft to the touch, and it should either lie flat or be slightly wavy. It should not be tight or curly. The feathering is on the ears, feet, and legs, and on the pants of the hindquarters. The long coat should have a large ruff on the neck, and the tail should be well feathered and carried like a plume.

Obviously this coat is going to require more work than the smooth coat, so it is essential that you accustom your puppy to being groomed on a table from an early age.

- A bristle brush should be used all over the body. Start working from the front of your Chihuahua, and progress along the line of the neck, over the body, to the hindquarters. If you progress in a logical order, you will not miss any areas.
- You will need to groom your dog's undercarrriage. You can stand your Chihuahua on his hind feet to do this, or you may find it easier to work with your dog on your lap, letting him lie on his back.
- Pay particular attention to the feathering, particularly behind the ears, and on the pants (britches), where it is most likely to mat. It is best to work through these parts of the coat in layers, grooming your way right down to the skin.
- You will also need to comb through the feathering, which will mat and tangle if it is not groomed regularly. If you come across a mat or a tangle, try to tease it out gently so that you do not break the hair.

The long-coated Chihuahua will shed his coat, and this can be a frustrating time for the proud owner. Groom your Chihuahua every day at this time, which will, ideally, hasten the process by loosening dead hair.

## BATHING

Regular brushing is the best way of keeping a dog's coat clean, but there may be times when you really feel your Chihuahua needs a freshening up. When you have a dog that sits on your lap and likes to be carried, it is essential that he is both clean and free from odor. The long-coated Chihuahua will need bathing more frequently, particularly if you are showing your dog (see Chapter Seven: Seeking Perfection).

Fortunately, the tiny Chihuahua is easy to bathe, and can easily be accommodated in a sink. The best tip is to gather everything you need before getting your Chihuahua wet!

It is also important to groom your Chihuahua before you bathe him. This will get rid of dry dirt, and, if you have a long-coated dog, you can make sure he is free from mats and tangles. If you try to rub shampoo into a tangled coat, you will get into no end of trouble.

- Start by placing a rubber mat in the sink. This will keep your Chihuahua from slipping.
- Ideally, fit a shower hose to the taps, which will allow you to control the flow of water

and the temperature. Test the water on your hand, making sure it is lukewarm.

- Before your Chihuahua has his bath, you can plug his ears with cotton so that no water gets into them.

- Start by soaking the coat, making sure you keep the water well away from your dog's head.

- Apply the shampoo and work it into a rich lather. Make sure you use a shampoo that is formulated for dogs, or you could end up with skin irritations. You can use an insecticidal shampoo if you are not using other preventive treatment for parasites (see Chapter Eight: Health Care).

- Rinse the coat thoroughly, making sure you get rid of all traces of shampoo.

- At this stage, you can apply coat conditioner. Dilute the conditioner in a jug of water, and then pour it over the coat.

- Rinse thoroughly, and use a towel to soak up the excess moisture.

- You can then lift your Chihuahua from the sink, wrapped in a towel, and take him outside for a good shake.

- The coat can be towel-dried. If you have a long-coated dog, make sure you do not rub the coat, or it will tangle. The job will be made easier if you use a hair-dryer, making sure it is on a moderate setting.

- Groom your Chihuahua as you dry the coat. If you have a long-coated dog, this will take some time, because you will need to brush through the coat in layers and pay particular attention to the feathering.

## Dental Care

Toy dogs do not always have the best teeth. There is a tendency for the teeth to be crowded in the mouth, and they can be shallow-rooted, meaning they are more likely to fall out as the dog ages. It is therefore essential to work hard at keeping the teeth clean, to give your Chihuahua the best possible chance of remaining free from dental problems.

The baby (deciduous) teeth will be replaced by the adult teeth from four months onward. The gums may be sore at this stage, but it is important to keep a close check on your puppy's mouth to ensure that the baby teeth come out as the adult teeth come through. Sometimes, the baby teeth fail to drop out, and this can cause problems of overcrowding. If you are worried about your Chihuahua's teeth, take him to the vet for a thorough examination.

*Teeth-cleaning should be a matter of routine.*

Modern methods of feeding mean that most dogs are given a diet of soft food, generally in the form of a complete diet. This has many benefits (see page 70), but it means that the teeth are not given a lot of work to do. As a result, tartar accumulates on the teeth, and this can lead to gum infection and tooth decay. Teeth-cleaning is therefore a must, and the sooner your Chihuahua gets used to the routine, the easier it will be. There are many types of doggy toothpaste on the market, and they come in a variety of meat flavors.

- Start by getting your Chihuahua used to having his mouth opened (see Handling, page 40). When your dog cooperates, reward him with a treat.
- Then try holding the mouth open for a little longer, encouraging your dog to remain still. Reward with a treat.
- Put a little toothpaste on your index finger, and rub a little on your dog's teeth. Ideally, your dog will like the taste, and will be quite happy with the attention. Remember to praise your dog for his cooperation.
- When you move on to actually cleaning the teeth, you can use a long-handled toothbrush or a finger brush. Squeeze a little toothpaste on the brush and clean the teeth, using an up-and-down movement.
- To begin with, you may have to stop after a couple of minutes to reward your dog. But in time, he will get used to the routine and will wait for his reward at the end of the teeth-cleaning session.

## Ear Care

The Chihuahua has large ears, which are carried erect. This allows a good flow of air (unlike the drop ears of Spaniel breeds), and ear problems are kept to a minimum.

Check the ears to ensure there is no sign of dirt, discharge, or bad odor. If the ear appears red and inflamed, and your Chihuahua is scratching his ear or shaking his head, seek veterinary advice.

If the ear just appears to be a little dirty, you can wipe it with a damp wad of cotton. However, do not be overzealous in your attempts to clean, or you risk doing more harm than good. Never probe into the ear canal with cotton swabs, as you could very easily inflict an internal injury.

*Make sure the ears are clean and free from odor.*

*The eyes can be wiped to get rid of any debris.*

## The Eyes

The large eyes of the Chihuahua should be bright and sparkling. Consult your vet at the first sign of discharge, redness, or inflammation.

Some Chihuahuas develop tear stains on the face. This may be the result of a blocked tear duct, where excessive tears drain onto the face rather than through the nose as normal. Your veterinarian can diagnose this condition with a simple test.

However, some Toy dogs suffer from tear stains simply because their tear ducts are too small for efficient tear drainage. The tears are more likely to stain on light-colored coats. There are a number of proprietary products that you can use to help eliminate staining; it is a matter of finding out which is the most effective for your dog. Some stains are stubborn and refuse to be removed.

## Nails

The Chihuahua has small, dainty feet, and the nails should be neatly trimmed. If your Chihuahua exercises on hard surfaces, the nails may wear down naturally, but in most cases, you will need to trim the nails.

*The nails can be trimmed with guillotine nail clippers.*

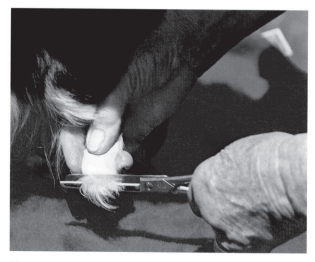
*If you have a long-coated Chihuahua, you will need to trim the excess hair that grows around the feet.*

*As a Chihuahua becomes older, his needs will change.*

When puppies are feeding from their mother, they knead at her belly, which can result in painful scratches. The breeder will therefore trim the puppies' nails with nail scissors. If you keep trimming your pup's nails, he will be quite happy with the procedure. It is far better to keep trimming a tiny bit from the nails, than to wait until they are long, by which time your puppy has forgotten all about nail-trimming.

As your Chihuahua gets older, you will probably find it easier to use guillotine-type nail clippers. Again, it is important to remove only the tip of the nail, or you risk cutting into the quick. This is not disastrous, but the nail will bleed, and your Chihuahua will probably build up a bad association with having his nails clipped. If you have a pale-colored Chihuahua with white nails, you will be able to see the quick. This is impossible with black nails, so you will need to be ultra cautious.

If you are worried about trimming your Chihuahua's nails, you can ask an assistant at your veterinary practice to show you what to do.

## THE AGING CHIHUAHUA

We are lucky that the Chihuahua is a long-lived breed, and that many dogs keep going well into their teens. Small dogs tend to stay young for longer than the bigger, heavier breeds, and many owners find their Chihuahua reaches double figures with few obvious signs of aging. However, it is inevitable that old age will catch up with your Chihuahua, and it is important to be aware of his changing needs.

In terms of exercise, you will probably need to make few changes to your routine – unless your Chihuahua was a great walker in his prime. The majority of older dogs will get as much exercise as they need in the yard. Their favorite occupation is lying down, watching the world go by, and then jumping up to bark a warning if strangers are approaching. If your elderly Chihuahua likes to be outside, it is a good idea to provide him with a bed, or some fleece bedding, so he has somewhere warm and dry where he can lie.

Even if your Chihuahua does not require much exercise, do not relegate him to a life

# OTTO THE GREAT

Otto can tell you all about landing on his paws. He was rehomed with Brenda Hayes when he was just over six months old – and 19 years later, he is still going strong…

Brenda and her husband, Mike, have had a Chihuahua in the family since the sixties, and now they share their home with six Chihuahuas, a Border Collie, and somewhere approaching 200 fowl. Brenda and Mike run a sanctuary for birds, and they care for chickens, guinea fowl, peacocks – and any other bird in need of a good home. However, there is no doubt as to who rules the roost – it's Otto!

At 19 years of age, Otto is surprisingly nimble on his feet, and he still boasts a full set of teeth. He enjoys all the comings and goings of his busy home – and he is totally loyal to Brenda.

"When Otto first came to us, he was very suspicious and unsettled," said Brenda. "The family he had been living with had split up, and no one wanted him. I suspect he was not very well treated, as he seemed to have lost his trust in people.

## EARLY DAYS

"I agreed to give him a temporary home while a permanent home was found, but I simply fell in love with him. I also realized that he needed someone who understood him."

Right from the start, Otto decided that Brenda was his special person. Mike, her husband, was tolerated, but as far as Otto was concerned, only one person mattered.

He accepted the other Chihuahuas, but generally preferred his own company.

"In his younger days, Otto's favorite place was snuggling inside a pajama case on the settee," said Brenda.

"But now, he has sorted out a place for himself. He moved into the cupboard under the stairs – and he regards it as his own den. He eats in there, and sleeps in there, and the other dogs are only allowed in by invitation. We call it his 'sheltered accommodation.'"

## TOP DOG

In his prime, Otto was very much top dog, and the other Chihuahuas clearly have a lot of respect for him. He has always had a great eye for the girls, and he is still quick to note when one of them is in season!

Otto suffers from arthritis, and is hard of hearing, but he takes a great interest in everything that is going on.

*Otto, age 19, is still going strong.*

## OTTO THE GREAT

"I let him please himself," said Brenda. "He sleeps when he wants to, and he goes out into the garden when he feels like it. Of course, I do pander to him. I always give him a treat with his food, and I have to be punctual with his mealtimes – he barks if meals are served late!

"Obviously, we can only live from day to day, but I will know when the moment comes and Otto is no longer enjoying his life. He may not have been the easiest of dogs, but he has given me total loyalty throughout his life – and there is no greater gift a dog can give."

*Brenda and Otto share a very special relationship.*

where he is always left behind. Take him for short outings, or for trips in the car, so that he still feels involved in what is going on – even though he does not wish to take an active part.

As your dog gets older, his dietary needs will change. The Chihuahua should never be fed too much at a time, and this is particularly true with older dogs. It is better to feed three small meals a day as your dog's metabolism starts to slow down. There are now many diets made specifically for veterans, and a transition to this type of diet will probably be beneficial.

Toy dogs are not blessed with the best teeth in the canine world, and as your Chihuahua gets older you will need to keep a close check for any signs of tooth decay or gum infection. If your Chihuahua is experiencing trouble with his teeth, you will need to consult your veterinarian before the problem gets any worse.

In all other respects, your Chihuahua will give little cause for concern – as long as he has a warm, cozy bed and plenty of attention!

### EUTHANASIA

Some dogs pass away in their sleep, but in the majority of cases, it is left to the owner to decide when their Chihuahua is no longer enjoying a reasonable quality of life.

As a dog owner, this is the hardest decision you will ever have to make, but it cannot be avoided. There is no kindness in allowing a dog to struggle on, coping with pain and loss of dignity, just because you cannot bear to say good-bye. When the time comes, try to arrange for your vet to come to your home, so that your beloved Chihuahua can let go in familiar surroundings, held by the person who has cared for him throughout his life.

Gradually, you will get over your grief, and be able to look back on all the happy times you and your Chihuahua spent together. Treasure the memories, and ideally, in time, you will be able to pay your Chihuahua the greatest compliment of all, and take on a new Chihuahua puppy…

## GOOD NIGHT, SWEET PRINCE

When Faith Maloney's beloved Chihuahua became terminally ill with liver cancer, she decided the kindest option was euthanasia. Here, she describes how she came to make that difficult decision.

"Prince Charming was two years old when I first acquired him. He was a tiny, six-pound black Chihuahua, who I adopted when his elderly owner was no longer able to care for him. Prince was taken to the Arizona Humane Society for re-homing, and he was featured on a special television appeal, which is how I found out about him. So many people called in to adopt Prince, the society held a lottery – I was the lucky winner.

"Prince was my first Chihuahua, and I didn't know much about the breed at the time. However, I knew I wanted a smaller dog, and he seemed perfect. Prince was impeccably well behaved, he was an adorable, affectionate character, and we bonded right from the start. Prince quickly became my best friend and constant companion, and we shared many happy years together.

"Once he was diagnosed with liver cancer, Prince's condition rapidly deteriorated. He couldn't make any red blood cells, and he was dying. My veterinarian explained what was happening to Prince, and that there was nothing that could be done to save him. I had to make a decision about euthanasia.

"I knew Prince did not have long to live, and I was no stranger to the wonderful gift of

**Prince was a wonderful dog, but Faith knew when his time had come.**

euthanasia at the end of life, but Prince was different. This tiny, little dog had made a big impact on my life and I was not ready to let him go. Prince was so special to me that I wanted to keep him for as long as possible. However, deep down I knew I would only add to his suffering if I did this. I opened up my mind to Prince, cuddling him and asking him, 'What should I do? I love you so much, I don't want you to die.' I don't know what I expected to hear back, but Prince looked at me as if to say, 'I'm ready to go. Don't keep me alive for your sake. It's my time.'

"Of course, I don't know if Prince actually 'said' those words to me, or if I was simply telling myself something I already knew, but the feeling of contact and communication with my wonderful Prince Charming was so intense, I knew euthanasia was the only option.

"Once I had made the decision, I called my veterinarian immediately – I didn't want Prince to suffer any more than he had to. Prince was my special companion, and his death was a great blow to me, but as he slipped away, I knew I had done the right thing. Animals teach us unconditional love, loyalty, and kindness. In my opinion, they make us better people. For our part, it is our duty to keep our pets free from unnecessary pain and suffering, and this is why I knew I had to let Prince go – hard as it was for me, it was the right choice for Prince.

"I've had many Chihuahuas since Prince, but he will always remain my special Prince Charming."

# CHAPTER SIX

# THE VERSATILE CHIHUAHUA

**T**raditionally, the Chihuahua has been viewed as a contented companion dog, happy to while away the hours on an affectionate owner's lap. However, despite his diminutive size, the Chihuahua possesses a larger-than-life personality, and his intelligence and friendly disposition make him well suited to further training.

The range of activities suitable for Chihuahuas is not as limited as you first may think, given the Chihuahua's size, and many sports can be adapted to suit smaller dogs. Indeed, the range of canine hobbies is now so extensive that there is something to suit almost everyone, depending on personal preferences, the dog's age and fitness, and the time you can devote to your chosen sport. By reading this chapter, you will have taken the first step toward a great deal of fun and fulfillment with your Chihuahua.

## CANINE GOOD CITIZEN

The "Good Citizen" program is an excellent starting point for anyone wishing to further their Chihuahua's initial puppy training and socialization. The UK Kennel Club runs the Good Citizen Dog Scheme, and the American Kennel Club equivalent is called the Canine Good Citizen Program. Both programs aim to encourage responsible dog ownership through education and training.

To receive his Canine Good Citizen award, your dog will need to demonstrate that he has been sufficiently trained and socialized to behave appropriately in a variety of everyday situations, including the following:

- accept handling and grooming
- respond to basic obedience commands
- meet another dog
- walk on a loose lead in a controlled manner

## DANNY DOES IT ALL

Pat Cullen has proved that Chihuahuas do have brains by training Danny up to the Gold Standard of the UK Kennel Club's Good Citizen Scheme.

After completing his bronze and silver tests, Danny had to be trained to a more advanced level to gain his gold award.

He had to complete the following exercises:

• walk on the road on lead
• return to his handler's side
• walk free beside his handler
• stay down in one place
• be sent to bed
• stop (instant Down)
• be relaxed when left alone
• show good manners over food.

Pat, who lives in Lymington, in the New Forest region of the UK, has been involved with Chihuahuas since 1983 when she established her Culcia kennel. She has bred a number of litters, and her dogs have enjoyed success in the show ring.

Danny, a long-haired red dog, looked promising as a puppy, but by six months it was clear that he was going to be too big for the show ring.

"It seemed such a shame to stop doing things with him just because of his size, so I decided to join a training club," said Pat. "There was a wide variety of breeds at the club – but Danny was certainly the smallest! However, that didn't worry him at all. Danny is so friendly, he does not believe he has an enemy in the world. He got lots of attention from everyone, so he was in his element."

At the training classes, Danny quickly showed an aptitude for learning.

"He is as bright as a button," said Pat. "He picks things up so quickly, and he is very keen on the treats he gets as a reward. He certainly believes in working for food."

*Danny loves a chance to perform.*

*Danny: Winner of the coveted gold award in the Canine Good Citizen Scheme.*

Danny sailed through his bronze and silver tests, so Pat decided to have a go at the gold.

"The only problem we had was during a training session when it was raining," said Pat. "I had to command Danny to go into the Down, but he didn't want to lie down on the wet grass. In the end, I was allowed to use a mat, and then he went into the Down without any trouble."

Danny's favorite exercise is the retrieve (although it is not required in the Good Citizen Scheme). Pat has taught him to retrieve a dumbbell (a tiny version, which is not too heavy for him to carry), and he has become most enthusiastic.

"We were at a training class where the majority of the dogs were Labrador Retrievers and Golden Retrievers," said Pat. "We were working on the retrieve and none of the retriever breeds could do the exercise. The instructor turned to me and said, 'At least we have one dog who can do a retrieve,' and she asked me to demonstrate with Danny. True to form, he did a lovely retrieve and got a round of applause!"

Pat has competed with Danny in a couple of exemption shows, but she is not planning to have a go at a higher level.

"The trouble with Danny is that he is so friendly," she said. "When he is off lead, he simply cannot resist going up to the steward to make friends – and if he sees a child in the crowd, he will be off in an instant to say hello."

Danny is not the only clever Chihuahua to get his gold award in the Good Citizen Scheme. Nicky, trained by Pam Kennedy-Minands, followed in his footsteps, and was awarded his gold the year after Danny.

"Chihuahuas love to use their minds, and it is a pity if owners neglect this side just because of their small size," said Pat. "The best thing about having well-trained dogs is that you really can take them everywhere with you, knowing they will do as they are asked."

- walk confidently through a crowd of people
- act confidently when faced with new or distracting situations
- be approached and petted by a stranger

If you have trained and socialized your Chihuahua as a puppy, he should not find any of these tests too difficult, but if your Chihuahua's behavior needs some improvement, try working on the exercises outlined in Chapter Four. You can also enroll in one of the many Obedience clubs that participate in the program, and that aim to prepare you and your dog for the tests.

## OBEDIENCE

If you enjoyed training and socializing your Chihuahua as a puppy, you may like to try Competitive Obedience. Chihuahuas are not well known as successful Obedience dogs, but there is no reason why the breed cannot perform well in this competitive sport. Indeed, the average Chihuahua is an alert and highly intelligent little dog – perfect for Obedience.

Having said that, training a Chihuahua for Obedience competitions is not easy, and requires a great deal of commitment and patience. If you are a highly competitive person, who likes to be the best and to win often, consider another breed for Obedience. However, if winning is not the be-all and end-all for you, and you think you would enjoy training and competing – as well as the obvious advantages of having an extremely well-behaved dog – then Obedience could be just the thing for you and your Chihuahua.

*The Sendaway exercise, where the dog must leave the handler and go to an allocated spot, is often trained using a mat to position the dog.*

If you think you may be interested in taking up Competitive Obedience, you will need to join an Obedience training club. The AKC will be able to provide you with details of clubs in your area.

### The Exercises

The exercises in Competitive Obedience vary slightly depending on where you are competing, but the basics are as follows. Of the following components, only heelwork and recall feature in the novice/beginners section – the rest are more advanced exercises.

**Heelwork**: Your dog is required to move beside you on the left side, both on and off lead, and to remain close (neither forward nor behind, but with his head level with your leg) whatever direction you take. Once your Chihuahua can walk in the correct position, and keep with you on left turns, right turns, and about turns, you can start to introduce changes of pace.

**Recall:** This exercise becomes increasingly difficult as you advance in training. A simple "novice" Recall involves putting your Chihuahua in the Sit, leaving him, and calling him in. The dog must sit in front of you, and then finish by coming to your left-hand side.

**Retrieve:** The dog must retrieve a dumbbell (in the advanced classes, any object chosen by the judge) thrown by the handler. Your Chihuahua must wait until he is given the command to "Fetch." He must pick up the dumbbell cleanly, and then return to sit in front of the handler in the proper position. The handler takes the dumbbell, and the exercise is finished when the dog returns to his handler's side.

**Distance Control:** The dog is positioned at a distance from the handler and must respond to a series of commands, which are given verbally, or by hand signals. The dog must move between the stationery positions of Sit, Stand,

# HARDWORKING HARLEY

Margie Ferguson, from Georgia, had always owned large breeds of dogs, namely German Shepherds. After acquiring a wonderful Pembroke Welsh Corgi, and achieving a great deal of success with him in Obedience competitions, Margie decided that her next breed of dog would be even smaller, and so she opted for the smallest breed of dog in the world.

"After my Corgi, Brett (Mystic's Redwick of Maren CDX) died, I took a break from dogs and Obedience for a few years. However, I really missed having some canine company and started to research various breeds of dog. I decided that a Chihuahua was the best choice for me, not only to fit in with my lifestyle, but also because I wanted the challenge of training such a small dog. Harley is my first Chihuahua, and he is now two years old.

"I have been interested in dog training since I was a little girl. Initially, I wanted to train Seeing Eye dogs for the blind, but, at that time, the Seeing Eye organization was based too far away. So instead, I decided to channel my energies into Obedience training, and the competition bug struck soon after.

## DAILY SESSIONS

"I was quite experienced in dog training by the time Harley came along, so it wasn't too difficult to start training him for Obedience competitions. I believe you should start training as soon as possible with any dog. You don't have to have long, regimented training sessions, but if you have small bursts of training every day, the dog learns to integrate everything he has learned into his everyday life, and he is generally much better behaved because of it. I have also found that short, daily training sessions have fostered a much stronger bond between Harley and myself.

"To begin with, Harley was very hesitant and unsure during training. However, although training made him nervous, the one thing he was not short of was courage. He would work with me no matter what, and, as time passed, he became more confident. I found that he was naturally good at heelwork (although, like every competitor, I think there is room for improvement). His willingness to be next to me helped him to learn this exercise very quickly. Now, Harley really enjoys himself, and his motivation to work just keeps getting better.

"One of the exercises we had problems with was the Recall. Harley had no problem understanding what he had to do, and he always responded to the commands, but his Recall was very slow – he would trot over to me in his own, slow time. The solution was found during our weekly group training class. We were practicing our Recalls in pairs, racing one dog against another. The only other small dog in the class was a Corgi called Gus – famous for his lightning-fast Recalls – so Harley was paired with him.

*Harley: A Chihuahua who thrives on the challenge of Competitive Obedience.*

## HARDWORKING HARLEY

"The first time we tried this, Gus raced towards his owner in his usual manner, but it was Harley's reaction that was great. The second he saw Gus speeding away, Harley was off – he made it from one side of the ring to the other in three seconds flat! With his long coat flying in the breeze, he looked just like a small rabbit in high gear! From that time on, Harley has always raced to me on his Recalls, whether we are competing or simply practicing at home.

### BIG ACHIEVEMENT

"Harley has competed in two separate, three-day-event Novice B Obedience competitions. He earned his AKC Companion Dog title in his first three shows, and his Obedience scores kept improving with every show. He was the only Chihuahua competing. Probably his biggest achievement was his performance at his last AKC Obedience Trial. He scored 193 out of a possible 200, which was a superb result.

"I've found that there is no reason why a Chi cannot learn Obedience just as well as a larger dog, but you must understand that the style of training needs to be different.

"For example, a larger dog will accept a correction, shake it off, and move on. However, Harley would be crushed if I scolded him too often or too severely.

"If Harley has difficulty with an exercise, it is best to abandon it for the moment and go back to it later, rather than persisting with it to the point where he loses all confidence and motivation. Instead, I use lots of praise and try to make each exercise as much fun as possible. Harley responds really well to this, and Obedience training has definitely had a huge impact on his confidence.

"Although Chihuahuas are not shy dogs, they benefit from the confidence Obedience training and competition gives them. They are constantly working around large dogs, which helps them to accept bigger breeds without fear – and when you're a Chihuahua, every dog is larger than you!

"Next on our agenda is to compete in the Open division of Obedience, once Harley is ready for it. It is more complex than the Companion Dog classes, and I am hoping that Harley will find it a lot more fun.

"After that, we may try Agility. One thing is for sure, no matter how much time or effort we need to put in, it will be well worth it. If you work hard with your Chi, he will reward you by becoming a loving friend and companion, a dog who you will be proud to take anywhere."

and Down, in whatever sequence is dictated, without moving from his original position.

**Sendaway:** This is where the dog is sent in a direction indicated by the judge, drops down at the owner's command, and is recalled in a certain direction (again, indicated by the judge).

**Scent Discrimination:** A series of cloths are laid out, and the Chihuahua must pick out the cloth with the judge's scent. In advanced classes, "decoy" scented cloths are also included to make the task more difficult.

**Agility:** In the United States, Obedience Trials also include an Agility section.

### FLYBALL

Flyball is a canine relay race that incorporates retrieve and hurdles. The sport is already extremely popular on both sides of the Atlantic, with more people taking it up every year.

Although the sport is dominated by Collies and Retrievers, Flyball has a proud tradition of many breeds of dog taking part, especially in the United States. Because of their size, Chihuahuas have to use their speed and accuracy, rather than relying on their ground-covering ability. They are unlikely to make it to competitive level because of their size, but you can still have fun with Flyball as a hobby.

Flyball involves two teams competing against each other on two identical tracks (each track is 51 feet or 15.5 meters long), and the winning team is the one that finishes first.

Each dog runs along a track, jumping over four hurdles on the way. At the end of the track is a Flyball box. The dog has to trigger the box to release a ball, catch the ball in his mouth, and then return to the start of the track, again jumping the hurdles on his return journey.

When the first dog returns, the second dog is released to run the course. This continues until all the dogs have run. If a ball is dropped, or if a hurdle is missed or knocked, the dog must run the course again after the last member of the team has run.

If you are interested in Flyball, you will first need to make sure that your Chihuahua is physically able to compete. Some of the tiny Chihuahuas are so small that they cannot trigger a Flyball box.

A number of clubs provide specially adapted boxes for smaller breeds, but very small Chihuahuas may find even these too difficult to operate with ease.

In addition, your little Chihuahua will not be able to cope with a full-sized tennis ball, and you will have to use a smaller version. Again, clubs with experience with smaller breeds should be able to offer advice on this.

To find out details of your nearest suitable club, contact the AKC.

## AGILITY

Agility is one of the most popular of all canine sports, and it is best described as an obstacle course for dogs. Each dog must successfully negotiate a series of obstacles, within a set time and with no faults. The winner is the dog that has the fastest time with the fewest mistakes.

The obstacles include hurdles, long jumps, tunnels and chutes, poles the dog must weave through, a seesaw or teeter-totter, a dog walk (a narrow, elevated walkway), and an A-frame (a steep, A-shaped ramp).

Agility competitions are usually full of breeds such as the Border Collie or Golden Retriever, but a small number of Toy breeds do take part, particularly in America. As with Obedience, you are less likely to win consistently if you compete with a Chihuahua (although there are exceptions), but there is no reason why your pet cannot be taught to perform well and give the bigger dogs a run for their money.

Agility is fun for dog and handler alike, and if competing at a high level does not appeal to you, you can stick to competing at lower-level club events, where the emphasis is more on fun than on winning.

**M**arian Stone never liked Chihuahuas, and certainly never considered owning one – until she was adopted by a long-coated male called Sunny…

"Sunny was a rescue dog," said Marian. "One of our neighbors works for the Humane Society, and when a long-coated, blond, male Chihuahua puppy was brought in, and none of the usual people were available to foster him, our neighbor asked us if we would mind caring for the puppy. At that time, Sunny was a complete mess. He was terrified of people and all too ready to bite. We had to work very hard to overcome his fear and control his biting.

"Sunny was only supposed to be a temporary addition to the family. We spent the first two months trying to find a suitable home for him. However, my mother tells me that she knew the night we brought Sunny home that he was going to stay, and she was proved right! Sunny stayed because I fell in love with him. I had never realized just how courageous and tenacious these little dogs could be.

"Most of all, I admired Sunny's indomitable spirit. He is a remarkably intelligent and independent dog, although he is totally devoted to me at the same time. He is cuddly and loving, and, as long as I am able to provide him with the right motivating reward, he will do anything for me. A friend of mine, who kept Chis in the past, once commented that Chihuahuas get very close to your heart, physically (due to their small size) and mentally (because of their lovable personalities). I think this describes my relationship with Sunny very well.

"Sunny's sad start in life meant that he had missed out on a lot of valuable socialization. My husband and I used to play Flyball in the past, and I thought it would be an ideal way to give Sunny some much-needed socialization. I had never seen a Chi run in Flyball, and I had no idea if Sunny would be any good at it, but I decided that I

would work with him if he showed some aptitude for the sport. However, my main reason for introducing Sunny to Flyball was to socialize him in a friendly environment, with lots of people who liked dogs, and, most importantly, people who had plenty of food in their pockets!

"Sunny was very easy to train, although this was probably helped by the fact that I had plenty of experience in Flyball. The key to training Sunny was to find the right motivation.

"Sunny has very little desire to do something simply to please me, but, with the right incentive, he can be taught to do anything – he is exceptionally bright. Fortunately, it wasn't too difficult to find Sunny's weak spot – food is his great motivator!

## MAKING PROGRESS

"I broke down Sunny's Flyball training into three areas. Firstly, I taught him to recall over the jumps, which he took to immediately. Secondly, I taught him how to retrieve the ball. Initially, I used a soft toy instead of a ball, backed up with treats as his reward for bringing the ball to me. Sunny was very good at running after the toy when I threw it out in front of him, but he was less good at picking it up and bringing it back to me. I had to work very slowly, reinforcing the idea that he had to bring me the toy before he could get the treat. Once he began to understand, I introduced tennis balls, although he cannot use a full-sized one. He can pick up a full-sized tennis ball if he really tries, but he can't hold on to it when he is running and jumping.

"Finally, I taught him how to trigger the Flyball box to get it to release the ball. This was probably the hardest thing for Sunny to master. Sunny is large for a Chihuahua, weighing in at 7.5 lb (approximately 3 kg), but even so, he had trouble with the trigger. He simply wasn't heavy enough. In the end, we had to get a box with a very light trigger, and if he doesn't pounce on it hard, it still will not release the ball.

"When we came to put all three areas of training together, Sunny mastered it very quickly. It only took six months to train him. However, it took a further six months before we could convince Sunny to perform in public. He found the crowds too intimidating. Today, though, he is quite at home performing demonstrations in public.

"One of Sunny's first public performances was a demonstration at our local university. Sunny had been running really well in practice, and I was eager to see how he would cope in a public place. I was feeling very confident, but when it came to Sunny's turn to recall over the jumps, he refused to budge. He acted as though the floor mats in his lane were dangerous.

"At first, I couldn't work out why the mats bothered him so much, especially as he was used to training on mats. However, I eventually worked out the problem. Where we practice, the entire floor is covered in mats. Sunny had never seen a single mat or a lane of mats before, with one exception – at home we have a 'scat' mat on our kitchen counter, to prevent Sunny from jumping up and stealing food. This was the only single mat that Sunny had seen. At the demonstration, Sunny was confused by the single lane of mats, and in his mind, I was asking him to play Flyball on a scat mat! I still chuckle about this every time I think of it.

"People frequently refer to Chis as having terrierlike qualities, and this is certainly true in Sunny's case. I can use his competitive streak to push him up a gear when we compete.

"He always runs faster in competitions than he does in practice, and I think this is because he is spurred on by the excitement that the other dogs show.

"Recently, this has really paid off. Sunny has just won his first Flyball title, in his very first proper tournament. He ran every race without penalties, and he actually became more motivated as the day wore on. When I think of the sorry state he arrived in, he really is a remarkable little dog."

---

## AGE CONCERN

Agility is a fairly demanding physical activity, for dog and handler alike. Consequently, you will need to ensure that you and your dog are fit and healthy before you take up the sport. For the same reason, national kennel clubs in most countries refuse to allow puppies or growing dogs to compete, as the demanding nature of some of the obstacles can damage growing joints. The AKC will tell you of the age restrictions in the United States, and give you details of Agility training clubs in your area.

---

### The Obstacles

Every obstacle appears huge to a tiny Chihuahua, and you will need to take this into account when training your dog. Many small dogs find the collapsible (cloth) tunnel quite scary, and the A-frame presents a much bigger challenge for the Chihuahua than it does for a German Shepherd, for example. That said, most Chihuahua owners who have taken up Agility find that their dogs love the sport. With the right training, all dogs can be taught to run the course to a very high standard.

However, because of the Chihuahua's size limitations, it is important that you seek professional help to Agility train your pet. Most Agility clubs affiliated with the AKC have qualified instructors, trained to a very professional level, and by joining an affiliated club, you will ensure that your Chihuahua receives the best training with the least danger to his health and mental well-being.

## CANINE FREESTYLE

Canine Musical Freestyle, or Heelwork to Music, is becoming increasingly popular as a dog sport. It began life as a form of Obedience, in which traditional Obedience exercises, such as Heelwork and the Sendaway, were performed to music.

However, the sport has grown to such an extent that many additional moves have been added, and today's performers incorporate turns, spins and jumps, so that handler and dog appear to "dance" in a well-choreographed performance.

Freestyle is very enjoyable to watch. It is extremely popular in the Unites States (where performances tend to be more flamboyant), and the trend is also beginning to sweep through the UK. There are numerous organizations involved with Freestyle, all with their own competition rules. However, generally, most performances last less than five minutes, and judging is divided into two areas:

- **Technical:** The synchronization between dog and owner, and the degree of difficulty in the routine, is assessed.
- **Presentation:** Costume, and the artistic flair shown in the choreography, are evaluated.

If you are interested in taking up Freestyle, you will need to develop a strong rapport with your Chihuahua, and he will need to be trained to a high standard of obedience.

Contact the AFC for more information on Freestyle organizations and how to get involved.

# MULTITALENTED DELIA

Ruthann McCaulley of Arizona has owned her Chihuahua, Delia, for two years. In that time, Delia has amazed everyone – including Ruthann and her husband, Raymond – with her incredible lust for life and all that it has to offer.

"We chose Delia because we knew that a Chihuahua would fit into our lives perfectly," said Ruthann. "At that time, we led a fairly sedentary lifestyle. We didn't want a large dog, as we only had a small yard at the back of our house. We also owned a Toy Poodle, who needed a 'sister' that wasn't so big that she would pick on him.

"We thought a Chihuahua was the perfect answer. However, since acquiring Delia and becoming involved in all of her activities, our sedentary lifestyle has become extremely active and busy!

## DELIA THE DANCER

"One of the first activities Delia became involved with was Obedience, and this laid the foundation for her other activities, including Freestyle. I saw a Heelwork to Music (the UK version) demonstration by Mary Ray at Crufts 2000, and thought it was the most wonderful thing I had ever seen. I knew I wanted to do that with my dog.

"It was very difficult to start because we live in a small town, and there was no one nearby who was involved with Freestyle. However, I managed to find a great book called *Dancing With Your Dog* by Sandra Davis, and that, along with training videos, got me started. Books and videos were the only tuition I had, but I've never been one who's needed a class to learn something new, so I read and reread the book, watched and rewatched the videos, and kept practicing a little every day.

"When I started to put together our first routine, I could tell that Delia was totally

*Delia soon got the idea of dancing with Ruthann.*

confused! We had been training the individual moves separately and she had no problem with any of them, but she didn't seem able to string them together. It was as if she couldn't make the transition from Obedience to Freestyle. I had to retrain her by combining a couple of moves together, and then building up to the whole routine. Delia is very intelligent, and it wasn't very long before she cottoned on to the idea.

"Although Delia is very quick to learn, we have to take training slowly. She can become bored quite quickly, so I have to keep training sessions short and fun, using lots of treats – Delia is totally food-motivated! Every night, after dinner, I use treats to get her to do 'dumb dog tricks,' which form the basis of a lot of her Freestyle moves.

## MULTITALENTED DELIA

"Training a Chihuahua to do Freestyle was not as difficult as I first thought, although I had to make allowances for her size. Delia doesn't like people bending over her, besides which, all that bending down kills your back. It also throws your body out of alignment, which can be confusing for the dog when you are trying to teach her to assume a certain position in relation to yours. A heeling dowel (rod) is an absolute must.

"Certain moves are not suitable for Delia because she is so small, but we try to take advantage of her size and make the most of the moves she can do. Because tiny dogs are naturally cute, I have to work quite hard to keep the routine serious, rather than 'cutesy.' A cute move is always a crowd-pleaser, and I throw in the occasional one, but if the whole routine is cute or comic, it can become 'old' very quickly, and it isn't a dance routine so much as a series of dog tricks.

"I've yet to compete in Freestyle with Delia, but she's not far off being ready. Our first routine, which was to *San Antonio Rose*, was very basic, but our current routine, to *Rhapsody in Blue*, is far more artistic and incorporates a lot more advanced moves. It's a lot harder for us both, but in many ways, it is also a lot more fun. Freestyle is quite demanding, and you certainly have to work hard with a Chihuahua, but the extra effort is definitely worthwhile.

### DELIA THE AGILITY QUEEN

"Delia's involvement with Agility grew from her Obedience training. I met a lady at Delia's Obedience classes who wanted to start an Agility group specializing in small dogs, and I jumped at the chance to become involved.

"Delia loved Agility from the very beginning. Her Obedience training was a great help in teaching her to focus on me and to listen to my commands. Agility gives the dog a lot more freedom than Obedience, and Delia responded to that very well.

*Delia soars over the hurdles.*

*The A-frame is Delia's favorite obstacle.*

*A confident run through the tunnel.*

"Initially, I began training her at home, making the obstacles from household objects. For example, our jumps consisted of a dowel rod propped up by two coffee cans! My son-in-law also made her a mini A-frame, which was great. Once we managed to train on the proper equipment, Delia really improved, and now we are taking private lessons, which is making a huge difference in our technique and training.

"Delia's favorite obstacle is the A-frame, although it's also the obstacle she finds the hardest, because of her size. She likes the view from the top and really enjoys sitting there and looking down at the world. I remember one competition we entered where she really got into A-frame mode. She enjoyed it so much, she did it three times! After that, she was just in it for the enjoyment, and refused to take it seriously. By the time she finished, even the judge was laughing at her antics.

"Delia's least favorite obstacle is the teeter (seesaw), which she hates. She does it, but the tip in the balance frightens her. She crawls her way along waiting for it to tip, and then creeps forward until it hits the ground. She refuses to hurry. During one competition, she was really slow on the teeter. Someone in the crowd shouted out, 'Keep going! Don't back up!' When Delia finally finished the course, a loud roar went up from the crowd, which was wonderful."

## DELIA THE THERAPIST

Ruthann's life revolves around her dogs, and she was eager to help those who were deprived of the comfort and companionship that dog ownership brings. She therefore decided to get involved in therapy work, taking her dogs to visit people in residential care.

"I started doing therapy work with my Toy Poodle, Boomer, after I saw a television program about therapy dogs and realized that Boomer was perfect for it," said Ruthann. "When Delia came along, she started accompanying

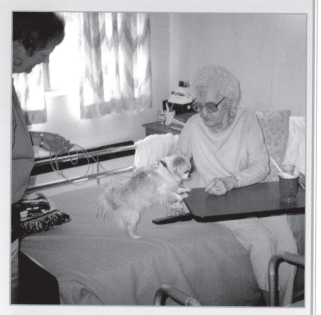

*Despite her hectic schedule, Delia still has time to bring comfort to people in need.*

Boomer on his visits and she took to it from the start.

"Therapy dogs must be really well socialized and have good manners. Delia has been to puppy preschool, puppy kindergarten, and basic obedience classes, as well as passing her Canine Good Citizen and TDI (Therapy Dog International) tests. She is ideally suited to therapy work.

"We visit a local care center for an afternoon once a week. The residents gather in a central area to play bingo and eat ice cream, so it is an ideal opportunity for us to reach as many people as possible. We also go around some of the residents' rooms.

"Delia loves the work, especially as she gets lots of treats. You have to watch a Chihuahua's weight, so I take along the treats for the residents to give to her, but occasionally she gets to lick out an ice-cream bowl! She loves performing her 'dumb dog tricks' to get everyone's attention, and she has learned to do them on a table so that she is high enough for all the residents to see her.

## MULTITALENTED DELIA

*Delia – a loving friend to many.*

"Delia has an uncanny knack of knowing which residents want her to sit on their laps so they can cuddle her, and which residents want her to sit so they can stroke her.

"When we go around the residents' rooms she stands at every door, sometimes going in and sometimes going on to the next door. It's as if she knows who needs her to visit that day, and who feels she would be intruding.

"Therapy work is probably the most rewarding of all our activities together. One time, we went to visit a stroke victim who couldn't talk or use her hands. She amazed everyone by reaching out to pat Delia.

"For many of the residents, seeing Delia gives them the opportunity to remember their own pets and to talk about them. Many of them are very lonely, so a visit from a dog and a chat with the owner really brightens up their day.

"Some of the residents can't speak, but they always smile and respond to Delia – even if they ignore everything else. I also find that residents

with dementia will often forget me, but they always remember Delia."

### DELIA THE PET

Summing up her pet's amazing versatility, Ruthann says: "Many people do not take Chis seriously, considering them to be cute, cuddly, useless little lapdogs. In fact, they are cute, cuddly, smart, and eager participants in just about any and every activity you could come up with.

"Obviously, you wouldn't rush out and buy a Chihuahua if you were burning to do Obedience, Agility, or Freestyle, but my advice to anyone who owns one of these wonderful little dogs is to rush out and give these activities a try."

Despite all Delia's achievements, Ruthann is most proud of her Chihuahua for her wonderful personality.

"Maybe Delia's greatest achievement is being a well-adjusted, confident, outgoing, loving companion and friend."

# CHAPTER SEVEN

# SEEKING PERFECTION

**W**hen you bought your Chihuahua, you may have had no more than a passing interest in the show world. But when you own a pedigree dog, you cannot help but become interested in the breed, and wonder why some dogs become Champions and others fail to make the grade.

Newcomers to the show world imagine that a judge looks at a line-up of dogs in the ring and then decides which dog they like best. This has an element of truth. The judge is making a personal choice, but his decision is governed by the stipulations of the Breed Standard. This is a written blueprint of how the breed should be in terms of appearance, movement, and temperament. It is the dog that, in the judge's opinion, most closely matches the Breed Standard that wins the honors.

## THE BREED STANDARD

The Breed Standard is drawn up under the auspices of the national kennel clubs, and there may be minor differences in the Standard, depending on where you live. The following description combines the main points of the English and the American Breed Standards.

## General Appearance

The Chihuahua is a dainty and compact little dog, noted for his saucy expression. This latter characteristic is open to interpretation, but a bold, slightly impudent expression is very typical of the Chihuahua's outlook on life.

## Temperament

Always on the alert, the Chihuahua should be friendly in his dealings with people and show no sign of nervousness. The American Standard states that the Chihuahua should have terrier-like qualities.

## Head

Typically, the Chihuahua should have a well-

*The Chihuahua is dainty and compact.*

rounded skull, with what is described as an "apple" dome. The cheeks and jaw should be lean, and the muzzle should be moderately short and slightly pointed. The stop, which is the step-up from the muzzle to the skull, should be well defined.

## Eyes

Set well apart, the eyes should be large and round, but they should not protrude. Dark or ruby-colored eyes are required, except in light-colored dogs, where a light eye color is permitted.

## Ears

The ears are large. They are held erect when the Chihuahua is alert, and when he is in repose they should flare to the sides at an angle of 45 degrees.

## Mouth

The jaws should be strong and meet in a perfect scissor bite. This means that the upper teeth closely overlap the lower teeth.

## Neck

The neck should be slightly arched, of medium length, and sloping into lean shoulders.

## Forequarters

The shoulders should slope into a slightly broadening support under straight front legs. The front legs should be set well under the chest to give freedom of movement.

## Body

If you took a line from just behind the neck to the tail-set, it should be level, and slightly longer than the Chihuahua's full height. The ribs should be well rounded but not too barrel-shaped.

## Hindquarters

Although the Chihuahua is such a little dog, he is well put together, and this is seen particularly in the hindquarters, which should be muscular and sturdy. The hocks, which are comparable to ankles, should be close to the ground, and should turn neither in nor out.

*The apple-domed skull is a unique feature of the breed.*

### Feet

As suited to a tiny Toy, the feet should be small and dainty, with the toes well split up but not spread. The pasterns, which are located on the front legs between the wrist and the toes, should be fine and springy.

### Tail

The tail should be of medium length, and set high over the back in the shape of a sickle. When the Chihuahua is moving, the tail should not be tucked under, or curled below the level of the back.

### Movement

The Chihuahua has a brisk, forceful action. The reach from the front legs should be equal to the drive from behind. The head should be carried high, and the line of the back should remain level.

### Coat

*Long coat*: Soft in texture, the coat can lie flat or be slightly wavy. There should be feathering on the ears, legs, and hindquarters. The neck should have a profuse ruff, and the tail should be plumelike.

*Smooth coat*: Soft in texture, glossy and close-fitting.

### Color

The Chihuahua can be any color or any mixture of colors. Currently, creams, whites, and fawns dominate the show ring. In the United States, you are more likely to see a range of colors and markings.

### Size

Size is judged in terms of weight. Both male and female Chihuahuas should not exceed 6 lb (2.7 kg). The American Breed Standard stipulates that dogs over this weight will be disqualified. The English Standard states a preference for dogs that weigh 2–4 lb (1–1.8 kg), and adds: "If two dogs are equally good in type, the more diminutive is preferred."

*Note the brisk, forceful action of the Chihuahua on the move.*

In fact, the size stipulation does not truly reflect the majority of dogs that are shown in the ring. Over a period of time, the Chihuahua has become a slightly bigger dog, and most dogs are 4 lb or over. This is entirely for the good of the breed, as the bigger dogs seem to have fewer health problems compared with the tinies.

The Chihuahua is not weighed at ringside, so the judge must rely on his own evaluation of weight and size. Obviously, it is important that the smallest breed of all does not lose its unique status, but it is equally important that the Chihuahua be a fit and healthy breed.

### Faults

In the UK, faults are universally classified as any departure from the points that are outlined in the Breed Standard. In the United States, a Chihuahua can be disqualified if he has certain faults:

- any dog over 6 lb
- a dog with broken-down or cropped ears (Cropped ears have been trimmed to make the ears erect – this is not allowed in the UK for any breed.)
- a cropped or bobtail – this is a tail that has been docked
- in long coats, a coat that is too thin so that it looks bare

### THE PURPOSE OF SHOWING

Why show your Chihuahua? If you have a top-quality dog, it is great to receive honors and admiration, but there is a far more serious side to showing.

*The judge's task is to find the dog that conforms most closely to the Breed Standard.*

If pedigree dogs were produced without judging them against a Breed Standard, it would not take long before you would see a variety of types. Dogs might get bigger or smaller, they may have small ears, or they may not have the distinctive Chihuahua movement. Soon, the breed that was developed hundreds of years ago would be lost in a hodgepodge of small, indistinguishable dogs.

If we are to preserve the Chihuahua, we must produce dogs that conform as closely as possible to the Breed Standard. The dogs that win in the show ring carry a great responsibility, because they will be the animals that are used for breeding. It is vitally important that they carry the true characteristics of the breed, and are sound in mind and body.

## SHOWGIRLS

Jacqui Beth Johnson, from Florida, acquired her first Chihuahua in 1975. She so loved the breed that, in 1988, she began breeding and showing Chihuahuas. Since that time, she has had a hugely successful showing career.

"My very first Chihuahua was a delightful fawn-and-white bitch called Shanti," said Jacqui Beth. "She lived with me for 11 years, and, although she was kept as a companion, she taught me to love the breed so that I knew I would have to have another. As I like to put it, Shanti 'Chihuahua-ized' me. Being so small, Chihuahuas tend to have a great deal of physical contact with their owners, and the bond between dog and owner becomes very strong, very quickly.

"After Shanti passed away, I decided to breed Chihuahuas, and managed to acquire a small number of high-quality dogs to found my kennel.

"Showing Chihuahuas can be quite a challenge. Chihuahuas are bred to be companions, and companion dogs often appeal to single people who have little contact with other people or dogs. When this happens, there is a danger that the dog and owner can form too strong a bond, which results in a Chi that is nervous around strangers and other dogs, and at worse, aggressive. Of course, proper socialization can overcome all these problems, but it needs to be consistent and taught from a very young age.

"One of the nicest things about showing Chihuahuas is that they are a lot easier to prepare for the show ring than some of the larger breeds. Chis are small and portable, and they do not need an awful lot of grooming. I think of them as a 'wash and wear' breed when it comes to preparing for a show.

"I began breeding and showing my dogs in 1988. I have always preferred to show my own

*Jacqui Beth Johnson wins Best of Winners with Ch. Tiffany at the Florida AKC dog show.*

dogs, rather than have a professional handler do it for me.

"To date, I have bred and shown 13 American Champions, but my proudest moment has to be when I was awarded the Bred-by Medallion. American shows contain a Bred-by-Exhibitor Class, which allows breeders who own and handle their own dogs to compete against each other. Most breeders consider it a great honor to win in this class, and one of my bitches, Ch. Anika's Felicity Foxtrot ('Tiffany'), achieved her Championship status in five shows, purely in the Bred-by class. This is why I was awarded the Bred-by Medallion. It was my biggest-ever thrill.

"I am currently showing Tiffany's daughter, Anika's Felicity Magic Mardi Graz, who won a five-point major in the Bred-by Class in her very first Specialty Show. I have extremely high expectations of her, and hope to continue showing for many years to come."

## THE ART OF BREEDING

The aim of a breeder is to produce a litter of fit, healthy puppies, and the hope is that one or two individuals may have the quality to compete in the show ring.

Put like that, it does not sound too difficult. If you mate a top-quality dog with a top-quality bitch, there should be no problem. Unfortunately, it is not quite as easy as that. When you are matching a male and a female, it is not enough to consider what they look like, what their temperament is like, and if they are both sound and healthy. Each dog is the product of generations of breeding, and may carry characteristics from ancestors that go back many years.

The skillful breeder has to research the bloodlines of both dog and bitch to be sure there are no outstanding faults running through either family. This should include a thorough investigation into health records. There are some inherited conditions in the breed, and it is essential that these be eliminated from any breeding program. (See Chapter Eight: Health Care.)

### LEAVE IT TO THE EXPERTS

If you have a pet dog, do not be tempted to breed from her. Breeding is an art form, and should be done only by experienced breeders with show-quality dogs. Great damage can be done to the breed by breeding indiscriminately, which can result in poor-quality puppies that nobody wants.

It is essential to use a brood bitch that is physically capable of carrying puppies. This can obviously be a problem in a tiny animal. Generally, the bitch should weigh a minimum of 4 lb; she should have a wide pelvis, and not be too narrow at the back end. It is important to find out whether females in the line are "self-whelpers," and can deliver puppies without needing a Caesarean. If a female needs a Caesarean, it is highly likely that her daughter will also have whelping difficulties. Obviously, puppies can be successfully reared after a Caesarean, but the mother is at considerable risk. A tiny dog such as the Chihuahua is very difficult to anesthetize, and it is a procedure that should be undertaken only when strictly necessary.

Now comes the most difficult part. The breeder has discarded dogs that clearly have faults, but what about producing puppies that are as good as their parents, or perhaps even better? The aim is to try to find a male and female that will complement each other, cementing the good points and improving minor faults. For example, if a female did not have the best ear carriage, you would look for a male that was strong in this department.

Generally, there are three types of breeding programs used in the dog world:

- inbreeding
- outcrossing
- linebreeding

## INBREEDING

Inbreeding is the breeding of two very closely related dogs, such as two dogs with the same father (sire). This type of breeding can be used when you want to accentuate – very quickly – a particular trait associated with the family.

Inbreeding should not be attempted by the novice. It requires the skill of experienced breeders who know the detailed histories of the dogs involved, and who will proceed only if they are confident that the resulting offspring will be strong and healthy, as well as being typical specimens of the breed.

*Ch. Dachida's Master Angel: A Champion produced as a result of inbreeding.*

| Parents | Grandparents | Great-Grandparents | Great-Great-Grandparents |
|---|---|---|---|
| Ch. Dachidas Jonnie Angel | Sventras Super Blue | Ch. Allende See Threepio | Maelake Imperial |
| | | | Allende Ava Maria |
| | | Sventras Sunbeam Golden Lace | Sventra Sundance Calico Kid |
| | | | Sventras Sunbeam Karis |
| | Dachidas Queen Bee | Ch. Arrendene Aggressor | Arrendene Spycatcher |
| | | | Arrendene Floral Lady |
| | | Chudor Florentina | Ch. Allende See Threepio |
| | | | Sumarchi Cornelia of Chudor |
| Dachidas Shadow Dancer | Dachidas Dancing Bear | Ch. Dachidas Jonnie Angel | Dachidas Queen Bee |
| | | | Sventras Super Blue |
| | | Dachidas Dancing Queen | Ch. Totsdown Tyson at Nikitos |
| | | | Yetagen Yarika |
| | Dachidas Queens Ransom | Ch. Arrendene Aggressor | Arrendene Spycatcher |
| | | | Arrendene Floral Lady |
| | | Chudor Florentina | Ch. Allende See Threepio |
| | | | Sumarchi Cornelia of Chudor |

## OUTCROSSING

Outcrossing is the mating of totally unrelated dogs, who have no relatives in common.

It is a method of introducing new blood to a line, and if you produce the result you are hoping for, you can go on to fix the type by linebreeding.

*Hamaja Elfie May was the result of an outcross mating, designed to bring new blood into the kennel.*

| Parents | Grandparents | Great-Grandparents | Great-Great-Grandparents |
|---|---|---|---|
| Gestavo Bravado | Belmuriz Brilliant at Marchez | Ch. Belmuriz Brevier | Ch. Apoco Ballybroke Billy Bunter |
| | | | Yaverland Playella |
| | | Belmuriz Royalinda | Ch. Belmuriz Royal Romance |
| | | | Belmuriz Brevina |
| | Gestavo Meconopsis | Arrendene Ariston of Trymside | Ch. Arrendene High Time |
| | | | Arrendene Top Love |
| | | Gestavo Maid Marion | Trymside Panchito |
| | | | Cleome Eve |
| Hamaja Hawthorne | Buster Brown of Hamaja | Ch. Hamaja Mappa Mundi | Ch. Allende See Threepio |
| | | | Hamaja Ruth |
| | | Mzdee Williams Girl | Matrish Lucky Star |
| | | | Mevagissey Miss Scarlet of Mzdee |
| | Hamaja May Blossom | Hamaja Matador | Ch. Hamaja Mappa Mundi |
| | | | Hamaja Pascale |
| | | Hamaja Jonquil | Ch. Danny Boy of Trymside |
| | | | Hamaja Roberta |

## LINEBREEDING

Linebreeding is similar to inbreeding in that it involves members of the same family, but they are not so closely related.

This is the most commonly used breeding program, as it retains the virtues of the line but also introduces new blood into a kennel.

*Ch. Dachida's Johnnie Angel: A linebred Champion.*

| Parents | Grandparents | Great-Grandparents | Great-Great-Grandparents |
|---|---|---|---|
| Sventras Super Blue | Ch. Allende See Threepio | Maelake Imperial | Ch. Maelake Mastermind |
| | | | Marlake Penelope |
| | | Allende Ava Maria | Myavon Blue Boy of Gilmay |
| | | | Kelitos Bonnie Belle |
| | Sventras Sunbeam Golden Lace | Sventra Sundance Calico Kid | Ch. Constanthorpe Jason at Taris |
| | | | Yaverland Minnie |
| | | Sventras Sunbeam Karis | Diella Topper |
| | | | Yaverland Elli Bianco |
| Dachidas Queen Bee | Ch. Arrendene Aggressor | Arrendene Spycatcher | Ch. Ballybroke Miles Better |
| | | | Arrendene Sibella |
| | | Arrendene Floral Lady | Arrendene Myman |
| | | | Arrendene Zoraya |
| | Chudor Florentina | Ch. Allende See Threepio | Maerlake Imperial |
| | | | Allende Ava Maria |
| | | Sumarchi Cornelia of Chudor | Ch. Rumawill Peter Piper |
| | | | Hamaja Honey of Sumarchi |

## PUPPY TO CHAMPION

A breeder can use all their expertise and experience to plan the "perfect" mating, but there is no such thing as a certainty when you are breeding pedigree dogs. To the layperson, a litter of Chihuahua puppies looks irresistible, but it takes years of experience to spot a Champion in the making.

Some breeders claim they can tell if a puppy is of show quality almost from the moment it is born. Others prefer to wait a little longer before making a choice!

The basic structure of the head and skull will alter very little, and by the time a pup is two weeks old, the typical apple dome should be apparent. The pup should have large, dark eyes, and big ears. At this age, the puppies' ears will still be folded; they will become erect when the pup is around eight weeks of age.

The Chihuahua is known as a "head breed," meaning that the head, with the apple dome, the large, lustrous eyes, and the big ears are entirely typical of the breed, and rate as the most important characteristics. In the show ring, a Chihuahua must have a good head to be successful.

Most breeders will wait until the litter is eight weeks old before making a final evaluation, because by this age, the pups will be on their feet and moving freely.

The pup with show potential should look strong, sturdy, and balanced. His body should be compact, and he should not be too long in the leg. Although the Chihuahua is a tiny dog, he should look completely in proportion.

### TOP TIP

A good rule is to look at a Chihuahua and say: "If this were a big dog, would he look balanced, and in proportion?" If the answer is "no," then your Chihuahua is not of show quality.

An experienced breeder will develop an eye for what qualities to look for, but pups can always surprise you.

A pup who shows great potential at eight weeks may not develop as well as expected, and, by six months, it may be clear that the dog does not have a future in the show ring.

Equally, a pup who showed no promise and was sold to a pet home may become a show-stopper.

Then there is the "ugly duckling" phase, when a pup with great potential goes through a bad patch. This can often happen with males, who may "go off" during their junior stage between twelve and eighteen months. Then, it is a matter of keeping faith and hoping the pup will mature into a beautiful Chihuahua. Generally, long-coated Chihuahuas seem to go through more changes than the smooth-coated type.

In both long-coated and short-coated varieties, the Chihuahua must have a presence that says, "Look at me." A dog that has natural showmanship is highly valued.

The following photos show the development of a Chihuahua from a tiny puppy through to maturity when the dog became a Champion.

## PUPPY TO CHAMPION
### CH. TEOCALI DESERT FLAME (Brumas)

*Brumas at six weeks.*

*Now age four months.*

*At twelve months, Brumas was awarded Top Longcoat Puppy in the Our Dogs—Pedigree Chum competition.*

*A stunning Champion, at three years of age.*

*The show dog must pose to show himself to his best advantage.*

## SHOW TRAINING

If you are planning to show your Chihuahua, you will need to give him special training. To the uninitiated, it may look as though all you have to do is take your dog in the ring and make sure he looks his best. But it is not as easy as it looks!

A show is an incredibly busy place, full of dogs, exhibitors, trade stands, and snack bars. Loudspeaker announcements blare out across the show ground, and every so often there is a round of applause as awards are handed out. The show Chihuahua has to take all this in stride and still walk into the middle of the ring as though he does not have a care in the world.

The key to training a show dog is socialization. Take your Chihuahua puppy out as much as possible so that he learns to get used to a wide variety of different sights and sounds (see page 39). In this way, your Chihuahua will mature into a calm, well-behaved dog, who is ready to take all new situations in stride.

You will also need to train your Chihuahua to perform in the show ring. The best plan is to find a club that specializes in ring training. This has a number of benefits:

• Your Chihuahua will meet and be socialized with other dogs. He will also learn to focus on you, despite other distractions.
• You will be given advice on how to pose your Chihuahua to his best advantage, and how to move him in the ring so that he shows off his gait.
• Your Chihuahua can be handled by different people so that he learns to accept the judge's examination.
• You will meet like-minded people, who will be able to give you the benefit of their help and expertise.

## Show Pose

The show Chihuahua must learn to stand in show pose. This means he must stand four square, looking completely balanced, so that the judge is able to assess his conformation.

There are different styles of showing, depending on the breed of dog. In the Chihuahua show ring, the tradition is to walk the dog into show pose. This is usually achieved by baiting the dog with food, although some exhibitors prefer to use a toy. When the dog is standing in position, he must focus his attention on his handler, looking as bright and alert as possible. Again, food is the answer with most Chihuahuas.

Obviously, it is quite a strain for a dog to maintain a show pose, so keep an eye on the judge. Pose your dog when the judge is looking in your direction, but give your dog the opportunity to relax when the judge is examining other dogs.

## On the Table

The judge will examine each dog in turn. This is often called the "hands-on" examination, as the judge will literally go over each dog so that he can assess all points of the Breed Standard. This will include looking at the dog's dentition, and, in the case of a male, checking to see if he has two descended testicles. Obviously, this involves quite an invasion of privacy, so your Chihuahua needs to accept all-over handling without resentment.

Work at keeping your Chihuahua's attention, while allowing room for the judge to examine the dog without interference.

## On the Move

The judge will then want to see how your Chihuahua moves. He will be looking out for the brisk, energetic action that is typical of the breed. An experienced judge will also be looking at how the Chihuahua is put together, which is revealed when a dog is on the move.

In the ring, exhibitors use a show lead, which is a very fine slip lead. This does not mask the dog's appearance, but the handler is left with minimal control. The show Chihuahua must learn to gait at a trot alongside his handler, neither pulling ahead nor lagging behind. He must turn neatly, and come back to show his movement from the front and from the side.

## Practice Makes Perfect

It takes many months of training before a Chihuahua is ready to be exhibited in the ring. Even then, a youngster may well act up and refuse to perform on the day. Be patient, and give your dog lots of encouragement. Be ready to reward him for good behavior, and never punish him for messing around.

A show dog needs to be full of confidence, and if you upset him, you may find that you have a Chihuahua that is a world-beater, but refuses to show himself off to the judge.

Remember, showing should be fun for both you and your dog. Enjoy your moments of success, but be sporting when it is not your day. Win or lose, you will be taking the same dog home with you – and that is the most important consideration of all.

Shirley Orme has been involved with Chihuahuas all her life – and as far as she is concerned, no breed equals the charms of the world's smallest dog.

"I just love them," she said. "They are so cheeky, and so full of life. They may be small, but they make wonderful guard dogs, and they are so loyal. For me, this is the breed that has it all."

Shirley started breeding Chihuahuas, but to begin with, she was not involved with the show world. "People came to see my puppies, and everyone said I should show my dogs," said Shirley. "I was worried that my dogs could pick up diseases at shows, but I decided to have a go. Within six months, nine of my puppies went down with parvovirus. This was in the eighties when the disease was at its height, and everyone was losing puppies. I didn't go to bed for a week. I stayed up and nursed the puppies, and in the end I managed to save five of the pups.

"Funnily enough, it did not put me off showing. In a sense, the worst thing possible had happened, and I had survived, so I felt I would always be able to keep my head above water."

Shirley's determination was rewarded when one of the first dogs she took to the ring – Cinders Glass Slipper – won a Challenge Certificate. Soon after this success Shirley established her Ormestex kennel – and she has been winning ever since.

"I established my kennel by linebreeding, and my greatest aim is to produce dogs of quality," said Shirley. "Of course, you must have a sound dog, but there is no doubt that the Chihuahua is a head breed. If a dog does not have the typical apple dome, large ears, and big eyes – it is not a Chihuahua. Breeding stock should also be 100 percent sound in temperament."

Shirley breeds both long coats and smooth coats – and is equally fond of both varieties.

"I like a dog to be pretty," she said. "You can get that with both long coats and smooth coats, but with a smooth coat, the dog has to be top quality. There is no coat to hide the faults."

Shirley's all-time favorite Chihuahua was a long coat called Miss Beautiful. She started showing Miss Beautiful and her brother, and when the pair were around 14 months of age, she decided to concentrate on showing the male.

"Beauty was a lovely dog, and when she was five and a half, I was persuaded to take her back into the ring," said Shirley. "By the time she was six, she was made up a Champion, and then she went on to win Best in Show as a veteran."

Shirley is currently campaigning three promising dogs – a long coat called Ormestex Forester, a smooth coat called Ormestex Frosty, and another smooth coat called Ormestex Victoriana. To date, Forester has won Best Puppy in Show at the Midland Chihuahua Club Show, and he got his first CC at the South Wales Kennel Association Show. Frosty took Best Puppy in Show at the Smooth Coat Championship Show, and won Best Puppy in Show on two occasions.

***Shirley with Ormestex Forester: A promising prospect in the show ring.***

"At the moment, I am just hoping for the best," said Shirley. "Frosty in particular is, to me, pure Chihuahua. He is the result of careful breeding over many years, and I am thrilled with him. But there is no such thing as a certainty in the show ring."

# CHAPTER EIGHT

# HEALTH CARE

The Chihuahua may well be the world's smallest dog but that is not his perception. Dainty and compact, this friendly, alert little dog is swift-moving. There is no doubt he thinks he is a big dog, which can lead to problems at times. For example, in practice, I found that broken limbs were often the result of jumping from a lap to a floor that just happened to be uncarpeted.

First, we begin with preventive care. This involves more than just ensuring that your pet has the right shots at the right time.

## PREVENTIVE CARE

Responsible preventive care involves
• an adequate vaccination program,
• comprehensive parasite control,
• controlled exercise, sufficient to satisfy this active dog's needs; otherwise obesity and all its attendant health risks can result. However, do not overexercise. In the young animal, this can result in joint and bone abnormalities.

• grooming: There are two varieties, shorthaired and longhaired Chihuahuas. Grooming involves not only brushing and combing, which even the shorthaired variety requires, but also attention to ears, eyes, teeth, and so on. This often averts major problems in the future.
• training: Although quite happy to act as lap-dogs, Chihuahuas are alert, swift-moving, forceful little dogs who need training. They are highly intelligent and therefore relatively easy to train. This should start as soon as you take possession of your puppy.

## VACCINATION

Vaccination or inoculation (and throughout this chapter the terms are used synonymously) stimulates the dog to produce active immunity against one or more diseases without developing any symptoms of that disease. In order to achieve this, the causative microorganisms (bacteria or viruses) have to be altered. They are either killed (inactivated) or weakened (attenuated) sufficiently so as not to cause the disease but to stimulate a workable immunity.

The altered microorganisms can be introduced into the body by various routes. For example, vaccination against kennel cough (infectious bronchotracheitis) is by the administration of nasal drops. Inoculation, on the other hand, usually involves an injection.

Irrespective of the method, the body produces an active immunity that lasts a variable time without boosting. This depends on the type of vaccine and the disease.

### Do puppies have any immunity at birth?

Puppies are usually born with some immunity that they acquire from their mother while still in the womb. The necessary antibodies are carried in the blood and cross the placenta into the puppy. This acquired (passive) immunity soon wanes, which is why vaccinations are necessary.

*Puppies acquire initial immunity from their mother.*

One of the main aims of vaccine manufacturers is to develop vaccines that will confer solid protection in the shortest possible time, even when circulating maternal antibodies are present. Canine vaccines are available today that can be completed by ten to twelve weeks of age, affording the puppy early immunity. This allows much earlier socialization and training.

### What about boosters?

Vaccination does not give lifelong immunity. Reinforcement (boosting) will be required. Recent work shows that the amount of immunity conferred varies with the disease, and is also determined by whether the vaccine is attenuated or inactivated. Generally, killed vaccines last a much shorter time; therefore boosters will be required. The problem is when to administer them.

Modern canine vaccines cover several diseases with one course of injections. This is for reasons of cost and convenience. Some components, however, particularly inactivated (killed) vaccines, such as the one against leptospirosis (kidney disease), are known to confer only a short immunity, often measured in months.

With any combined (multivalent) vaccine, the efficacy of the product as a whole is considered in relation to the component that gives the shortest period of effective protection. Therefore, although protection against diseases such as distemper and hepatitis will last for much longer than a year, because these are combined with leptospirosis, the manufacturers' recommendation will be that an annual booster of the multivalent vaccine is advised.

*Booster vaccinations can be discussed with your vet.*

### Is there any truth about bad reactions to boosters?

Recent concern regarding the possibility of some dogs developing reactions to booster vaccination has led to a rethink, and manufacturers' recommendations are beginning to change.

Primary vaccination and boosters are now tailored for the individual and the area. Discuss this with your local veterinary surgeon at the time of the primary vaccination.

There is concern that problems, particularly those of an autoimmune nature, can be caused by overvaccination, particularly "overboosting." I think this risk exists, but is considerably smaller than the risk of these killer diseases reemerging should we allow our pets' immune status to fall dangerously.

### Can immunity be measured?

Blood tests are available, both for puppies and adult dogs, that will accurately indicate whether immunity has fallen to a level where the dog is at risk and boosting is advised. However, the cost of testing for one disease will probably be equal to, if not more than, the cost of a combined revaccination for all the diseases. Economics apart, there is also the question of stress for the dog.

Venipuncture, to obtain a blood sample, is likely to be resented far more by the dog, particularly one as tiny as a Chihuahua, than a simple subcutaneous shot to reinforce immunity against all the diseases.

Because of the concerns expressed regarding vaccination, the number of components combined in each injection, and the recommendation of annual repeats, vaccines have recently been divided into two groups: **core vaccines** and **noncore vaccines.**

**Core vaccines:** These are the necessary vaccinations that protect against diseases that are serious, fatal, or difficult to treat. In North America, these include distemper, parvovirus, hepatitis (adenovirus) disease, and rabies. In the UK, rabies is not a core vaccine, but this may change now that quarantine regulations have been amended. In North America and Britain, veterinarians are unanimous in advising protection against the core diseases.

**Noncore vaccines:** In Britain and North America, noncore vaccines include those against

Bordetella and leptospirosis. In the United States, Coronovirus and Borellia (Lyme disease) vaccines are added. This latter vaccine in particular is known to cause a reaction. Which noncore vaccines are used depends upon a risk assessment for the particular animal. This should be discussed with your veterinarian.

Bordetella vaccination, for example, via the administration of nasal drops, gives only approximately six to nine months of immunity. It is valuable if your Chihuahua is going into boarding kennels or attending training or socialization classes, but may not otherwise be considered necessary.

Discuss these and any other problems with your veterinary surgeon during those all-important primary inoculation visits. Primary inoculation is considered to be sound, preventive medicine, as is the first annual booster when the pup is about 15 months of age. Future vaccinations will depend upon the advice of your local vet. Many factors influence this, including local infection levels, breed susceptibilities, and so on.

## CANINE DISTEMPER

Canine distemper is no longer widespread in most developed Western countries, solely because of vaccination.

Signs (symptoms) include fever, diarrhea and coughing, with discharges from the nose and eyes. Sometimes the pads harden, and this is the so-called "hardpad" variant. A significant proportion of infected dogs can develop nervous signs, including fits, chorea (twitching of muscle groups), and paralysis.

Because of vaccination, distemper is seldom ever seen in the United States and Britain today. This leads to a false sense of security. The virus is still out there, waiting for its opportunity. This was demonstrated in Finland only a few years ago, when a serious epidemic of distemper occurred solely because of falling levels of immunity in the canine population.

## HEPATITIS

Hepatitis is also known as adenovirus disease. Signs range from sudden death in serious cases to mild infection where the dog only appears to be a bit "off-color." In severe cases, there is usually fever, enlargement of all the lymph nodes (glands), and a swollen liver.

During recovery, "blue eye" can occur. This is caused by swelling of the cornea (the clear part of the front of the eye). The dog looks blind. Although initially very worrying, this usually resolves quickly without problems.

## PARVOVIRUS

Parvovirus is caused by a virus that is particularly stable. In other words, the virus can exist in the environment for a long time. The disease reached epidemic proportions in Europe and North America in the 1980s. Main signs include vomiting and diarrhea that is often bloodstained (dysentery).

The rapid development of safe, effective vaccines brought the disease under control in Western countries, although it is still a serious killer, rivaling only distemper in many other parts of the world.

*Dogs in the USA must be vaccinated against rabies.*

### RABIES

Rabies vaccination is compulsory in many countries, including the United States. In Britain, it may well become so, after the relaxation of quarantine laws (all imported dogs have to be vaccinated).

The virus is spread by bites from infected animals, often foxes, bats, raccoons, and skunks.

### PARAINFLUENZA

The parainfluenza virus is considered to be the primary cause of kennel cough syndrome, referred to as infectious bronchotracheitis in North America. In the UK, *Bordetella bronchiseptica*, a bacterium, is considered to be the main cause.

A component against parainfluenza has been incorporated in multivalent vaccines for some years.

The manufacturers recommend annual vaccination against parainfluenza with the suggestion that, if your dog is going into a high-risk situation, such as boarding and attending shows, even earlier revaccination should be considered.

The disease, like Bordetellosis, is not usually life-threatening except in very young and very old dogs.

The signs are a persistent cough, and infection can last longer than symptoms. This carrier state is how the disease becomes rife.

### BORDETELLOSIS

Kennel cough syndrome, infectious tracheitis, infectious bronchotracheitis – a variety of names are used for a disease that can spread very quickly when animals are closely congregated.

Chihuahuas with tracheitis are really pathetic. They can cough persistently for up to three weeks but seldom seem to be particularly sick. However, recent work has shown that there are very virulent strains of Bordetella that cause serious disease with the onset of rapid bronchopneumonia.

Unlike the parainfluenza vaccine, Bordetella is not incorporated into the usual multivalent vaccines. It is usually administered separately via nasal drops. These have been shown to give better immunity than conventional inoculation.

In Britain, there is a combined parainfluenza and Bordetella intranasal vaccine available.

## LEPTOSPIROSIS

Leptospirosis is unique among the multivalent vaccine components since Leptospira organisms are bacterial and not viral in origin. Two forms (serovars) are combined into Leptospira vaccines. *Leptospira canicola* is mainly spread in the urine of infected dogs, whereas with *Leptospiral icterohaemorrhagiae*, rats are the main vectors.

Recent work has shown that dogs infected with leptospirosis invariably reveal strains other than *L. canicola* and *L. icterohaemorrhagiae*. Since these latter are zoonotic, that is, communicable to man, this is one of the reasons that vaccination is still recommended.

However, since it is a killed (inactivated) vaccine, the Leptospiral component is probably the shortest-acting of all the various components in multivalent vaccines. Because manufacturers' recommendations regarding vaccination are based upon the shortest-acting component, questions are raised as to whether its inclusion is really necessary.

Again, discuss this matter with your vet.

### CANINE CORONOVIRUS

This virus can cause diarrhea, particularly in puppies. The disease is usually mild and responds to supportive therapy. A vaccine is available in North America and some European countries, but no licensed vaccine is currently available in Britain.

## LYME DISEASE (BORRELIOSIS)

The bacterial Lyme disease is carried by certain ticks whose bite can transmit it to dogs and man. It is very common in parts of North America and does occur in the UK. It causes widespread acute arthritis. This polyarthritis affects dogs and people. Fever, heart, kidney, and neurological problems can also occur.

Although vaccines are available in North America, there is currently no licensed vaccine available in Britain, although cases of Lyme disease occur in the UK.

## PARASITES

Parasite control is an important part of preventive health care and is essential for all dogs, irrespective of size or lifestyle. Parasites are roughly divided into two groups:

- **Ectoparasites** live on the surface of the host and include fleas, lice, ticks, and mites.
- **Endoparasites** live within the host. Worms are the most well known, but there are other equally important endoparasites such as coccidia and giardia, although these may not be quite so widespread.

## FLEAS

Fleas are the most common ectoparasites on the dog. They are found worldwide, and Chihuahuas, whether smooth- or long-coated, can pick them up from the environment or from contact with other animals.

Some dogs will carry a very high flea burden without problem, whereas others will show

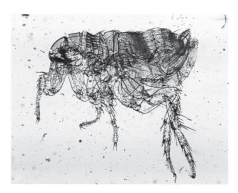

*The dog flea – Ctenocephalides canis.*

evidence of typical flea allergy dermatitis (FAD) although no fleas can be found. This is caused by the development of a hypersensitivity to flea saliva.

FAD is not common in the Chihuahua but it can occur, causing serious pruritis (itching) with considerable hair loss.

Fleas are not host-specific, and infestation of many Chihuahuas can be traced to the family cat. All types can bite us as well as a range of other animals.

Effective control involves both adult fleas on the dog, and the immature stages that develop in the home. Fleas need a meal of blood to complete their life cycle. The adult flea then lays eggs on the dog. These soon drop to the ground. Provided the temperature and humidity are within the correct range, they develop into larvae (immature forms) in the carpets or gaps between floorboards. Development can also take place outdoors, as long as the temperature and humidity are correct.

Under ideal conditions, the life cycle can be completed in as short a time as three weeks. In suitable conditions, fleas can live without feeding for more than a year. This is why dogs and people can be bitten when entering a property that has been left unoccupied for some time.

**FLEA CONTROL:** There are many effective preparations to control adult fleas on the dog. Sprays and prolonged-action spot-on preparations are probably the most effective.

Adult fleas account for only approximately 5 percent of the total flea population. Control of the other 95 percent, consisting of immature stages, can be much more difficult. Few environmental insecticides have any effect against immature fleas, so an insecticide with prolonged action should be used. This will be effective against any subsequently emerging adults. Control in the home should also involve thorough vacuuming to remove any flea larvae.

Oral preparations are also available that, given to your dog, will prevent the completion of the life cycle of the fleas. The compound is transferred to the adult flea when it bites the dog for the all-essential blood meal.

Insecticidal baths are useful for killing any adult fleas seen in the coat, but they do not have a lasting effect. Therefore bathing should always be combined with other methods of flea control to reduce rapid reinfestation.

Most small dogs dislike flea sprays, mainly because of the noise. In such cases, spot-on preparations should be considered. The chemical, which is lethal to the flea, is dissolved

 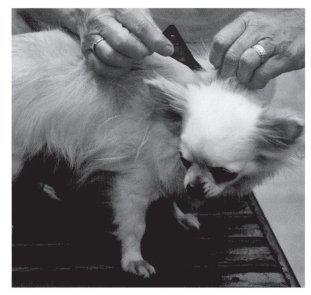

*Flea infestation can be controlled by using a spray (left) or by using a spot-on treatment (right).*

in a vehicle that spreads through the invisible fat layer of the dog's skin. Within 24 hours, the dog will have total protection against fleas for approximately two months.

When the flea bites the dog for the all-important blood meal, it has to penetrate the fat layer to get to the blood supply, and, in so doing, ingests the chemical. If the dog gets wet or is bathed, the efficacy of the treatment is not affected. However, it is important to reapply the preparation according to the manufacturer's recommendation (usually every 30 or 60 days) to ensure complete protection. Some preparations are also effective against certain endoparasites, particularly roundworms.

### LICE

Lice are not usually too much of a problem in the Chihuahua. They usually require direct contact for transmission, and, unlike fleas, the whole life cycle occurs on the host. The eggs (nits) are attached to individual hairs. Infestation is usually associated with violent itching and often affects the head and ears.

Bathing in an ectoparasitical shampoo is effective treatment. Close contact between dogs is necessary to spread the parasites; therefore they are not uncommon in dogs or puppies acquired from puppy farms (puppy mills).

### TICKS

Ticks are carriers of various diseases, including Lyme disease (Borelliosis). Babesiosis and Ehrlichiosis are other tick-borne diseases found in the United States.

Several flea and lice preparations are effective for tick control. Your veterinarian will advise you on the best choice.

## CHEYLETIELLOSIS

*Cheyletiella yasguri*, the causal mite, can just be seen by the naked eye as a tiny white speck, hence the term "walking dandruff." The condition is not uncommon in puppies acquired from large kennels or from puppy farms (mills). The mite causes intense irritation. I have seen it occasionally in smooth-coated Chihuahuas that have been impeccably reared.

The mite is zoonotic and can cause intense irritation, particularly in children. In kennels, the mite is spread by adult dogs who are themselves symptomless. Treatment with any of the ectoparasitical preparations results in rapid cure. Obviously, other pets should be treated to ensure that reinfestation does not recur.

## HARVEST MITES (CHIGGERS)

Chiggers are the larvae (immature forms) of a mite that lives in decaying organic matter. They are red in color and just visible to the naked eye. They can be picked up by dogs exercised in fields and woodlands, particularly areas with a chalky soil. The muzzle and head, as well as the dog's feet, can be affected.

Any of the usual insecticidal sprays or washes are effective, but reapplication is necessary if you live in an area where the larval mite is rife. Problems usually occur in autumn.

## MANGE

Mange is a parasitic skin disease caused by microscopic mites. Two types of mite can cause the disease in dogs, **demodectic** and **sarcoptic** mites. In my experience, I have not found that mange is a particular problem in the Chihuahua.

**DEMODECTIC MANGE:** Demodex mites live in the hair follicles and sebaceous glands of many normal dogs and cause problems only if the host becomes immuno-incompetent for any reason. It is for this reason that demodectic mange is not thought of as a contagious disease in the same way as sarcoptic mange.

If the demodex mite starts to multiply, signs including inflammation and hair loss are seen. Secondary bacterial infection then can be a problem.

Veterinary treatment using modern preparations is effective once a positive diagnosis has been made.

**SARCOPTIC MANGE:** Sarcoptic mange is zoonotic. It is known as scabies when it occurs in humans; children are particularly susceptible. Often, intensely itchy areas develop on their arms and abdomen as a result of nursing the affected dog or puppy.

Modern veterinary treatments are effective, but diagnosis sometimes requires repeat skin scrapings. If you are concerned, contact your veterinarian.

## ENDOPARASITES

There are a number of endoparasites that affect dogs, but you will find that worms are the most important as far as your Chihuahua is concerned. Protozoan parasites, such as Coccidia and Giardia, may also be a problem in certain areas, particularly in North America.

## ROUNDWORMS OR NEMATODES

Until relatively recently, roundworms – particularly in puppies – were considered ubiquitous. More knowledge of the complex life cycle, together with the development of modern roundworm remedies, have resulted in a dramatic reduction in the number of worm-infested dogs and puppies.

The most common roundworm is **Toxacara canis**. It is a large, round white worm 3–6 inches (7–15 cm) long. The life cycle is complex. Puppies can be born with toxocariasis acquired from their mother before birth. Do not forget the fact that the worm is the same size, no matter whether it infests the bowel of a Great Dane or your tiny Chihuahua.

Roundworm larvae can remain dormant in the tissues of adult dogs indefinitely. In the bitch, under the influence of hormones during pregnancy, they become activated, cross the placenta, and enter the puppy, where they finally develop into adult worms in the small intestine. Larvae can also be passed from the bitch to the puppy during suckling.

There are now many safe and effective worm treatments available. Endecticides are spot-on preparations similar to those used for flea control, but they contain drugs such as selamectin that are effective not only against fleas but also roundworms and heartworms.

Preparations are available today that are licensed for use in puppies – even tiny Chihuahua puppies from 14 days of age. Many preparations are available over the counter, but you are advised to seek veterinary advice on the

*Regular worming for roundworm is essential in young puppies.*

worming program for your Chihuahua. This is important, especially with puppies, since a regular worming program should be undertaken for long-term effective endoparasite control. Your vet will advise you.

There is a slight risk of roundworms being transmitted to humans. It is important that you ensure your Chihuahua remains worm-free. In general, treatment is recommended only if a fecal examination reveals that worms are present.

## TAPEWORMS OR CESTODES

The tapeworm is the other common type of intestinal worm found in the dog. They differ from roundworms in that they do not have a direct life cycle, so spread is not from dog to dog but has to be through an intermediate host.

This varies according to the type of tapeworm. Intermediate hosts include fleas, sheep, horses, rodents, and sometimes humans.

In the dog, the most common type of tapeworm is **Dipylidium caninum**. This worm, which can be quite large, up to 20 inches (50 cm), uses the flea as the intermediate host. The worms live in the intestine, and eggs are contained within mature segments. These look like grains of rice when shed from the end of the worm and passed out into the dog's feces.

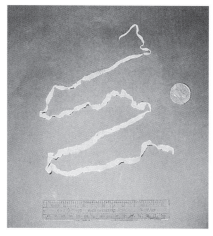

**Tapeworm passed by an adult dog. (The coin gives an indication of size.)**

Free-living flea larvae eat these microscopic eggs, which mature as the flea matures. When the adult flea is swallowed by a susceptible dog, the life cycle of the tapeworm is completed. Like roundworm remedies, effective tapeworm remedies are widely available without prescription. However, effective eradication involves vigorous flea control, including the developing flea larvae in the environment. Therefore, it is a wise strategy to seek veterinary help.

There are other types of tapeworm more common in larger dogs with an outdoor lifestyle. The intermediate hosts are rabbits, hare, and similar wildlife, which they catch and eat.

Tapeworms of **Echinococcus species** are important in dogs in general because of their zoonotic potential. Dogs are generally infected only by eating raw, infected meat. The risk for your Chihuahua is therefore relatively small.

With the introduction of the PETS program in Britain, any dogs entering the country have to be treated with specific remedies against **Echinococcus multilocularis,** which can cause serious cysts in the lungs of people. Thus, it should be borne in mind that, if you travel abroad with your Chihuaua from Britain, treatment against this tapeworm is mandatory on reentry – even though the risk of your dog being infected may be very small.

## HEARTWORM

*Dirofilaria immitis* or heartworm causes major problems in many of the warmer parts of the world, including North America. It is the deadliest worm in the United States, and is responsible for many dogs' premature deaths.

Transmitted to dogs via the mosquito, the heartworm larvae moves around the bloodstream, eventually reaching the heart. Here, it can take hold and block up the heart – with devastating results.

Selamectin, mentioned previously, is one of the effective drugs available. Consult your vet if heartworm is a problem in your area.

## OTHER INTESTINAL WORMS

Hookworms (*Uncinaria* and *Ancylostoma* species), together with whipworms (*Trichuris vulpis*), are occasionally the cause of lack of condition and more severe signs such as anemia or dysentery.

These worms are more of a problem in large kennels. The worms are often discovered during routine fecal investigations rather than because of illness.

Treatment is uncomplicated with modern de-wormers prescribed by your vet.

## GIARDIA AND COCCIDIA

Giardia and Coccidia, microscopic protozoan endoparasites, can cause diarrhea problems, particularly in puppies. Giardia is a water-borne disease, more common in North America than in Britain. The disease can be a problem in the UK in imported dogs. This is likely to increase with the relaxation of quarantine regulations.

*Responsible owners should learn the principles of first aid.*

Giardiasis is considered to be zoonotic, and is the most common intestinal parasite in humans in America. Nevertheless, there is no conclusive evidence that cysts shed by dogs and cats are infective to humans.

If you are concerned, a simple stool test is available.

## EMERGENCY CARE AND FIRST AID

For small dogs such as the Chihuahua, all sorts of emergencies can occur – bites, burns, broken legs, heat stroke, insect stings, poisoning, and scalding, to mention but a few. These can all happen without warning.

First aid is the initial treatment given in such an emergency. The purpose is to preserve life, reduce pain and discomfort, minimize the risk of permanent disability or disfigurement, and prevent further injury.

## EMERGENCY PROCEDURES

Irrespective of the cause, in any emergency there is a certain protocol, which is worth observing.

- Keep calm and do not panic.
- Get help if possible.
- Contact your veterinarian, explain the situation, and obtain advice specific to your circumstances.
- If there is possible internal injury, try to keep the patient as still as possible. With a dog the size of a Chihuahua, it is a good idea to place him in a cardboard box or some other makeshift container, ensuring that he is safe and secure. The dog should then be taken to

the veterinary clinic as soon as possible.

• Drive carefully and observe the speed limits.

Depending on the nature of the emergency, it may be necessary to carry out first aid on site. Following a sequential routine is the most efficient approach. This is observing the A, B, C of first aid.

**A is for Airway**: This means checking the dog's mouth and throat, and ensuring that there is no obstruction preventing air from reaching the lungs.

**B is for Breathing**: Check to see if there are signs of breathing.

**C is for Circulation**: Make sure the heart is beating.

For example, if the dog is choking because there is something lodged in his mouth or throat, try to remove it before doing anything else. Take care! Remember that the most docile, affectionate pet in such a situation will be terrified. Use a stick or some other implement if you have to dislodge anything in the mouth; otherwise you are in danger of being bitten.

Once the airway is clear, check for breathing. Place the palm of your hand around the dog's chest, just behind the forelegs. Can you feel a heartbeat, and is the chest moving? If there is no movement of the ribs, and you can feel no heartbeat (pulse), artificial respiration and cardiac massage can be easily combined in a dog the size of a Chihuahua.

The heart is situated in the lower part of the chest, just at the level of the elbows. With your hand around the sternum, fingers on one side and the thumb on the other, start gently squeezing approximately twenty to twenty-five times a minute. This has the dual function of stimulating the heart and helping to get air into the lungs. About every 10 squeezes or so, check for a heartbeat or any breathing. If you manage to start the heart, continue for several minutes. This is cardiopulmonary resuscitation (CPR).

Check the color of the mucous membranes of the gums or under the lip. When you first started, it was probably white or ashen-gray. Once the heart is beating, a vague pink tinge should return. This return of color will be very subtle because the dog will be shocked.

## SHOCK

What is shock? Shock is a complex condition disrupting the delicate fluid balance of the body. It is always accompanied by a serious fall in blood pressure. Causes include serious hemorrhage, heart failure, heat stroke, and acute allergic reactions, such as bee stings. Signs of shock can include the following:

• rapid breathing

• rapid heart rate

• pallor of the mucous membranes of the gums, lips, and under the eyelids

• sometimes vomiting

• severe depression

• a cold feel to the limbs, ears, and so on.

The most important first-aid treatment for shock is to keep the dog warm, but do not apply too much external heat. Wrap the dog in blankets, newspapers, clothes – whatever is available – and get him to your vet as soon as possible.

In the rest of this section, I am going to briefly outline first aid for some of the common emergencies that can occur with a Chihuahua. The list is by no means comprehensive, but knowledge of the common first-aid approach for these conditions should help when confronted with any emergency.

## BLEEDING

Quite severe hemorrhage can occur in Chihuahuas from torn nails, which, if they are too long, can catch in floor coverings. Torn nails and cuts on pads and limbs should be bandaged fairly tightly using any clean material. A plastic bag can then be bandaged on to the limb.

Bleeding from other parts of the body, including the head and ears, cannot be so easily controlled. In these cases, try applying a cold-water swab and finger or hand pressure.

## BURNS AND SCALDS

Burns and scalds can happen all too easily when the tiny, inquisitive Chihuahua gets in the way while you are cooking, or making a cup of tea or coffee.

First, cool the burned area with cold water as quickly as possible. If the acccident involves a caustic substance, such as drain cleaner or bleach, wash away as much as you can with plenty of cold water. Keep the area damp and get to your vet as soon as you can.

## EYE INJURIES

Chihuahuas have large eyes that are vulnerable to injury. Scratches from bushes and cats' claws

*The Chihuahua has prominent eyes, which can be prone to injury.*

are not uncommon, plus there is the problem of getting grass seeds under the lids.

Use a pad to apply cold water, or, better still, saline solution (contact lens solutions) to cleanse the eye. If the eyeball appears to be torn, or if there is any bleeding, try to cover it with a pad soaked in cold water, and take your dog to the vet as soon as practicable.

## HEAT STROKE

In warm, humid weather, heat stroke can rapidly occur. Ill-ventilated rooms, as well as cars, can be responsible. Remember, the dog need not necessarily be in the sun for the condition to strike.

The first signs are excessive panting with obvious distress. Coma and death can quickly follow because of irreversible changes in the blood vessels.

Reduce the temperature by bathing your Chihuahua in cold water, and place ice on the gums, under the tail, and in the groin. Take the still-wet animal to the vet as soon as possible.

## FITS AND SEIZURES

During a fit or seizure, your dog is unconscious and does not know what is happening – although it is pretty terrifying for any onlookers.

It is important to prevent injury while the dog thrashes about. If possible, place him in a cardboard box.

When the dog is coming out of the seizure, he is unlikely to be able to see or feel properly. If he is confined in a box, the risk of injury is greatly reduced. The container will also limit the amount of light around, and it has been found that keeping the dog in a subdued light hastens recovery.

The dog should come out of the seizure in a very few minutes, although it may seem much longer to you.

If the dog is still seizing after five minutes or so, telephone your vet for advice. Otherwise, wait until your dog is out of the seizure, and then take him, in his container, to the vet for a full examination.

## BREED-PRONE PROBLEMS

Many members of the Toy Group suffer breed-associated problems. As the smallest dog in the group, Chihuahuas, by and large, are probably the least affected of any. For example, dental problems are widely recognized in Toy breeds, yet the Chihuahua is less severely affected than the Yorkshire Terrrier or the Maltese, for example.

## HEART PROBLEMS

Heart problems can occur in many small breeds of dog, including some that are not Toys (such as West Highland White Terriers). Chihuahuas do have cardiac problems, particularly with advancing years. Often this is a right-sided enlargement of the heart, and concomitant congestive failure. The condition occurs more frequently in overweight, out-of-condition dogs.

There is a low incidence of hereditary heart murmurs – you should check with the breeder that their line is free from this condition before buying a dog.

## LUXATING PATELLA

Slipping kneecaps (luxating patellae) are basically joint problems. The kneecap moves in a groove at the lower end of the femur (thigh bone). Some dogs are born with a groove that is not deep enough so that the patella slips out of the groove, usually to the inside of the joint. This causes the dog to hop for a few steps.

If mildly affected, the kneecap will often return to its groove and the signs of lameness disappear. Sometimes, both legs are affected, and, particularly if the Chihuahua is overweight, the condition can be crippling. Often it first shows itself when the dog is as young as six to twelve months.

Today, there are very successful surgical techniques to correct the problem. Nevertheless, it is wise to refrain from breeding any affected individuals.

## HYDROCEPHALUS

Commonly known as "water on the brain," hydrocephalus is a condition in which excess fluid collects within the brain cavity of the skull.

*With good care and management, your Chihuahua should live a long and healthy life.*

It can be a result of trauma, for example a bang on the head, but in the Chihuahua there can be a problem with congenital hydrocephalus, meaning the abnormality may be present before or at birth.

The cause is not really known except that it is a developmental abnormality. It may be genetic in origin, but until DNA testing has been sufficiently developed, we cannot be certain. However, we do know that it is more common in particular breeds, of which the Chihuahua is one. Again, it is unwise to breed from affected individuals.

If the condition is mild, the puppy may just be a bit slow and less intelligent than the siblings. In more advanced cases, circling and pacing may occur, culminating in seizures and paralysis.

Today, modern imaging techniques can result in accurate diagnosis. Mild cases respond well to medical treatment aimed at reducing the intercranial pressure.

## CRYPTORCHIDISM

The testes (testicles) develop in the abdomen and gradually descend into the scrotum. They should be present there at birth, or shortly after. If they have not descended by the time the dog is adult, he can be described as either a unilateral cryptorchid (when one testis is still retained in the abdomen), or a bilateral cryptorchid (when both have not descended).

Chihuahuas are considered to be prone to this condition, although, in some late developers, the hidden testis may descend when the pup is about six months of age. Nevertheless, it is always worth checking with your veterinary surgeon at the time of vaccination. Affected dogs, even if only unilateral cryptorchids, should not be bred.

## SUMMARY

Like any dog, the Chihuahua can experience health problems, but if the correct preventive care is given and if regular checks are made, you should have a long-lived, healthy companion who will share your life for many years to come.

You may have the world's smallest breed, but you can guarantee that your Chihuahua will make a big impact on your life!